THE COURAGE TO LIVE

THE
COURAGE
TO LIVE

by
Ari Kiev, M.D.

THOMAS Y. CROWELL, PUBLISHERS
Established 1834   New York

THE COURAGE TO LIVE. Copyright © 1979 by Ari Kiev, M.D. All rights reserved. Printed in the United States of America. No part of this book may be used or reproduced in any manner whatsoever without written permission except in the case of brief quotations embodied in critical articles and reviews. For information address Thomas Y. Crowell, Publishers, 10 East 53rd Street, New York, N.Y. 10022. Published simultaneously in Canada by Fitzhenry & Whiteside Limited, Toronto.

FIRST EDITION

Designer: Eve Kirch

Library of Congress Cataloging in Publication Data

Kiev, Ari.
   The courage to live.
   Includes index.
   1. Suicide—Prevention. 2. Depression, Mental.
I. Title.
RC569.K53 1979   616.8′5844   78–69517
ISBN 0–690–01801–0

79 80 81 82 83 10 9 8 7 6 5 4 3 2 1

CONTENTS

Whatever enlarges hope will also exalt courage.
—SAMUEL JOHNSON

INTRODUCTION

Suicide: A Personal Problem, A Public Problem

Every year, tens of thousands of Americans take their own lives.

Estimates of the incidence of suicide vary because many suicides are not reported as suicides and it is difficult to ascertain whether certain deaths are accidental or self-inflicted. The most reliable figures, however, place the number of suicides in the United States at between 25,000 and 50,000 per year—with the number constantly on the rise. The number of *attempted* suicides, moreover, may run as high as 250,000 per year! Obviously, suicide has become a public health problem of major gravity.

What kinds of people kill themselves?

When we think of someone taking his or her own life, we commonly imagine a thoroughly isolated individual—a morose, friendless soul with "nothing to live for" and no reason left to keep trying. While this image may fairly accurately describe many suicides, it by no means gives a picture of the range and diversity of suicidal individuals. Suicide is a contemplated or realized option in every stratum of our society, among people in every age group, ethnic cluster, and religion.

People with serious emotional difficulties, alcoholics, and drug-dependent individuals are, not suprisingly, among the most common suicides. But there are also several other classes of people to whom suicide seems especially attractive. These include, ironically, both the very old and the very young.

In a nation where youth is exalted and age is conspicuously ignored, it's not unexpected that the neglected elderly should have high suicide rates. But, so the figures suggest, the dream of youth has provided little comfort to the young; suicide, shockingly, is the third most common cause of death, after accidents and homicides, among American adolescents. Approximately 5,000 people between the ages of fifteen and twenty-four will kill themselves in this country in this year alone.

In the past twenty years, the incidence of suicide among the young has increased to epidemic proportions. The suicide rates for teenagers (ages fourteen to nineteen) *doubled* between 1960 and 1970—as did the rates for males in their twenties. Among females in their twenties, the rates *quadrupled*. Among American Indian youths and young urban black women, suicide ranks *first* among causes of death.

Why this shocking rise in self-destruction? And what, if anything, can be done about it?

Suicide has only recently come out of the closet, so to speak, to become a possible topic of conversation. Since our research on the subject is still in the early stages, we still face many unanswered questions.

Is suicide, for example, caused by unhappy experiences in life or by a genetic mental imbalance? Is it an act of desperation or one of courage? Is it a radical response to distressing circumstances, or only a cry for attention? Most important, how can the people suffering from the kind of depression that commonly triggers suicide be helped to choose an alternative way of dealing with their unhappy situations?

From considerable scientific investigation over the past two decades, we now know much more about suicidal behavior. We know, for example, that few people who attempt suicide simply want to die. What they want is not to live *if* living means continued suffering.

We also know that depressive illness, which accounts for the vast majority of suicide attempts, is limited in duration and that it is a treatable condition. Yet despite such knowledge, and despite the availability of effective medications and a variety of psychotherapeutic and community mental health programs, the suicide rate in the United States has not declined.

There are complex sociological reasons for America's suicide problem. Mentioned among the causes have been the availability of lethal weapons, the effects of the "drug culture," and the general effects of such recent catastrophic events as the Vietnam War and the Kennedy and Martin Luther King assassinations.

Such examples of social malaise and disruption may indeed contribute to the prevalence of depression—as, of course, does the economic and political climate in general. A recent report of the National Institute of Mental Health, for example, noted a link between unstable economic conditions and a sharp rise in the treatment of mental illness, particularly depression.

But these economic, social, and political stresses do not *cause* depression and suicide. They merely *intensify the underlying conditions* in a depressed individual's life, and may aggravate them to the point where he or she "cannot take it anymore."

The real causes of suicide are personal, and the problem is really one of recognizing them before treatment is indicated. We must learn, for example, to differentiate symptoms of depression from normal reactions to everyday life stresses. We must learn to recognize how the many factors involved in an individual's depression—including the attitudes of friends and relatives, the presence of external life stresses, and the unwillingness to accept treatment—can all contribute to suicidal drives.

In this book I examine the specific personal factors that can push an individual to the brink of desperation. Understanding these personal factors can enable a potential suicide to change direction, renew courage, and find new meaning and purpose in life.

In the past fifteen years I have evaluated and treated some 2,000 depressed and suicidal patients in my own private practice, at the crisis intervention clinic I established at New York Hospital and at the Social Psychiatry Research Institute, in New York, which focuses on the development of new social and biological treatments for depression. In the course of this work I have found that, even when overwhelmed by seemingly insurmountable problems and obsessed by the desire to die, such patients *could* be reached. Once patients realize that there is a way to master distressing symptoms, through psychological counseling and drug therapy, many of them develop the initiative to solve their "unsolvable" problems and begin their lives anew.

In fact, for many potential suicides, the suicide crisis is a positive turning point. Once it is passed, they find that they can redirect their self-destructive impulses toward positive, self-renewing activities. The suicide attempt sometimes seems to break the depressive cycle, to push the patient not over the edge but into a clearer, more productive reflection.

It is my hope that this book will enlighten those who suffer or know someone who suffers from depression and that it will help retard the rising rate of self-destructive behavior in general, and suicide in particular. A suicide attempt is not the end of the line. Often, it can be the first step on a widening, healthier journey. Depression may be a principal public health problem, but it *is* curable. Perhaps public policy cannot easily eliminate all the aggravating factors in suicide. But we can identify the immediate, personal factors and provide effective therapeutic help.

1

Choosing to Live

Look well into thyself; there is a source of strength which
will always spring up if thou wilt always look there.
—MARCUS AURELIUS

Helplessness, apathy, and despair are feelings we have all
experienced. Do people who commit suicide, or attempt to do
so, experience such feelings with greater intensity or for longer
periods of time than other people? Do they reach a point
within despair where it begins to seem unalterable and permanent? Do they at that point see themselves as utterly powerless,
unable in any way to make the choices that can influence the
direction of their lives?

While it seems reasonable to suppose that the answers to
these questions would be yes, in fact the situation is not quite
so simple as that. It's often assumed that someone who takes his
or her own life has drifted into the final act in a kind of
mindless fog; suicide becomes, for such an individual, the only
thing left, something he or she falls into rather than consciously chooses. The cliché is that the suicide simply "gives up."

This view of the suicide as someone who has forfeited all
options is misleading, for in fact the person who tries to kill

himself or herself must make a very clear choice, must initiate a critical decision over the direction of his or her life.

It is important to keep this in mind, for by recognizing that a suicide attempt requires energy, direction, and choice, we will be better able to counsel both patients and their families to deal with a dangerous crisis. Suicides are not will-less, floating casualties. Indeed, suicide often requires considerable courage and determination. It involves marshaling energies toward a specific goal, and this implies that the suicide has, far from giving up on choice, actually made a definite choice—albeit a self-destructive one.

It is the therapist's task, therefore, to redirect energies, to show the potential or "failed" suicide that the choice of self-destruction is not the *only* choice—and certainly not the best one.

I have often said to patients referred to me after a suicide attempt, "If you have the courage to attempt to kill yourself, why not apply that courage to living your life as you want to live it? Pursue your *own* interests for a change. Stop giving in to the demands and pressures of others."

If you have the courage to die as you choose, you should have the courage to live as you choose.

Consider the case of a forty-one-year-old ex-seaman who visited my office several years ago in a state of severe depression. A tall, physically strong black man, Ted had been unemployed for some time because of a back injury and saw no immediate prospects for work. Disability insurance provided him with a meager income, but it was barely adequate to his needs, and this had become a cause of constant depression. In addition, his friends and strangers alike avoided him. Because of his imposing stature, he appeared angry and menacing when, in reality, he was withdrawn, shy, very depressed, and seriously contemplating suicide.

In treating Ted, I turned first to chemotherapy, prescribing an antidepressant that alleviated the symptoms of his depression. These included fatigue, insomnia, loss of appetite, sexual impotence, anxiety, and suicidal obsessions. The drug allowed him to begin functioning more normally and reduced the risk of suicide.

Then we began regular psychotherapy sessions.

When we began, Ted was preoccupied with failure. Since nothing he had done recently had turned out to his satisfaction, he had come to assume that nothing ever would. My first task, therefore, was to direct his attention away from past failures and convince him that there were still plenty of options open to him.

What those options were, of course, he would have to decide for himself. So the first order of business, after the antidepressant had made him more able to communicate with me freely, was to determine what, aside from failure, were his personal areas of interest.

"What do you like to do in your spare time?" I asked him one day.

"Oh, fooling around with wood, I guess," he admitted after some hesitation.

"You mean whittling or carving?" I asked.

"No, building things—like bookshelves."

I encouraged Ted to spend more time at woodworking. As it turned out, he was quite good at it, and so I suggested that perhaps he could make something more of it than just a hobby.

As treatment progressed and his symptoms began to disappear, Ted devoted increasing amounts of time to building furniture. He began to teach woodworking and cabinetmaking at a drug rehabilitation center, spending his nights dreaming up new designs. Soon he was making furniture—small tables, stereo cabinets, and the like—for other people as well as for himself. Before long, he found that the hobby had become a business, as he began to sell his work and became known as a reliable and inventive craftsman. Within a short time after considering suicide, he had found a purpose in his life from a quarter he had previously not thought of investigating. To his surprise he had uncovered that "source of strength" of which the Roman philosopher Marcus Aurelius spoke, and it had enabled him to choose to live.

And incidentally, to live well. Today, Ted runs his own renovating business. With a team of people working under his direction, he regularly grosses between $10,000 and $15,000 a month.

Before treatment, like many suicidal people, Ted had never considered the feasibility of making a living by doing what he *enjoyed* doing. Now he continually renews himself through his work. His business reflects *him* and is the product of his own unique gifts. Most significant, he is no longer depressed and has had no further thoughts of suicide.

Since many men define themselves through their careers, their suicidal crises tend to relate to their work experience. Among women, such crises are more often precipitated by personal relationships. Failed romances, loneliness, and feelings of isolation, of course, plague men as well as women. But statistically, the precipitants of suicide among women are more likely to be related to problems in love than to problems on the job.

Sharon, a suicidal woman of forty-four who recently entered treatment in my private practice described the conflict inherent in her turbulent relationship with a married man, on whom she was excessively dependent. Although she described the relationship as "hell," she also told me, "I can't leave him because, to me, it is more important to love than to be loved— even though every time we see each other there is friction."

This woman was a perfect case of the person who neglects his or her own interests and capacities in a mistaken effort to please another and thereby gain external approval. She had forgotten what she herself had, and could only define herself in relation to an obstructed and tense partnership. In therapy, I had to assist her to become more self-assertive so that she could begin to act independently for her own self-interest.

Another suicidal patient, Jennifer, was so afraid that her boyfriend would eventually reject her that she abdicated any life of her own and remained literally at his beck and call. Before making any plans, she would wait to hear from Jim. If Jim finally called at the last minute, Jennifer always managed to be "free," even if it meant canceling other arrangements.

When Jennifer and Jim did get together, especially after a week or more of separation, she always felt compelled to report to him on how, where, and with whom she had spent her time. She never complained when he failed to call as expected, for fear it might antagonize him and drive him away.

Inwardly, Jennifer raged at Jim for mistreating her, but since she was afraid to vent this rage, she turned it on herself, convincing herself that she was the one at fault and even that she deserved ill treatment. As she came to realize during treatment, these repressed, volcanic emotions provided the principal fuel for her suicidal fantasies.

Before Jennifer could develop the courage to live her own life, to become her own person, she had to learn to act in new directions, independent of Jim. With much encouragement on my part, she became increasingly able to resist the impulse to account for the time she spent without him. Less dependent on his plans, she gradually became less available to him.

The "new Jennifer" unsettled Jim. He became anxious, uncertain—and jealous. And with his interest in her thus rekindled, he proposed marriage.

Now, I do not mean to suggest that keeping your lover at arm's length is the best way to increase his or her ardor. Jennifer herself, I understand, is still weighing Jim's proposal, and has not yet determined that life with someone who took her for granted for so long is necessarily preferable to life alone. The central point, however, is clear: she was able to overcome her depression, to master her inclinations toward suicide, only after realizing that she had a choice about her behavior, that she could choose the direction of her life.

Jennifer's story is instructive on another count as well. It illustrates how a person can kill himself or herself in many ways short of actual suicide. Jennifer would not, I think, have put a gun to her head; yet her masochistic attraction to Jim served in a sense to make her die a little bit each day, to make her feel as if she deserved no better than this slow death.

This is a problem I will talk about later in the book. Actual suicide is really only the tip of a vast iceberg of self-destructiveness. Most people, even if they avoid contemplating suicide, have many difficulties in successfully living creative and purposeful lives. We all have problems in coping. We may never attempt suicide, but we are bound to commit countless "mini-suicides" in our daily responses to stress.

Some of us do this by becoming overly dependent upon alcohol, sleeping pills, or other drugs. Others of us become accident-prone or chronically late, thereby minimizing our chances for social or business success. Others provoke arguments with lovers and friends, thus effectively sabotaging personal relationships. And some of us merely climb into bed and stay there; while not so violent as suicide, such behavior is also self-destructive, and I will discuss it in Chapter 8.

For the time being, however, I want to concentrate on ways of dealing with actual suicidal tendencies. In the bulk of this book, I will discuss what I believe to be a sensible approach to this most severe type of self-destructiveness. Treatment, I believe, should involve three essential aspects:

1. The use of antidepressant medication, which alleviates the symptoms impairing normal functioning, and reduces suicidal thoughts and drives.

2. A program of psychotherapy, preferably involving the

family as well as the patient. Here, the goal is to improve the individual's life-style, bringing all of his or her resources to bear in overcoming those small acts of self-destruction that feed the depression.

3. A plan for crisis intervention in order to cope with external pressures that may push a patient back to the brink of despair.

In dealing with suicide, the four key tasks of psychotherapy, as I will discuss them here, are:

1. The search for the reasons behind the patient's problem. This means investigating ostensibly innocent pressures experienced by the patient at home and on the job. Often such pressures can appear so benign that the patient doesn't recognize them as stress-creating, and as a result internalizes the stress, making demands on an already over-wrought psyche. The first task of therapy, then, is to help the individual to recognize what it is he or she does *not* want to do—so much so that the patient would rather die than do it—and second, what the person really likes and *wants* to do.

2. The mobilization of energy. The recognition of pressures and the reduction of burdensome responsibilities liberates considerable time and energy. The second task then becomes an attempt to discover meaningful personal direction for the liberated energy.

3. The involvement of the immediate family. This can be of great value if the family members can learn to lessen their demands—both spoken and unspoken—on the patient.

4. Strengthening the patient's will. In addition to helping the patient to say no to those demands of others that do not serve his or her best interests, the therapist must finally be able to direct the liberated energy of the patient into an area that the individual can identify as important and self-renewing. Ideally, the end of this process is a situation in which the patient discovers within something he or she had missed before, and is animated by the discovery to a new appreciation of the possibilities of his or her life.

No one has ever lost everything. In moments of "ultimate" disaster, something remains. It is the goal of the therapist, and of the suicidal person, to uncover that something and nurture it into the foundation of new energies, new possibilities, new choices.

What the suicidal person must be urged to understand is that anyone with the courage to end his or her life can also develop the courage to begin it.

2

Signs of Depression

A railroad track toward hell . . .
—ANNE SEXTON, *Despair*

The symptoms of physical illness are generally much easier to identify and diagnose than those of emotional or mental disturbance. Such widespread diseases as cancer and heart trouble have received so much attention from the press and the medical establishment that their early warning signs are fairly well known to the layperson; as a result, they can often be identified and treated before serious damage is done to the constitution. Sadly, this is not the case with mental illnesses. Countless people suffering from mental problems—and depression in particular—are ignored or diagnosed too late to be of any help, partly because of shame or embarrassment on the part of the depressed individual.

This is an unfortunate outcome of the centuries-old view of mental disturbance as something fearful, shameful, and mysterious. In the Middle Ages, depressed individuals were generally thought of as "possessed" souls in league with the devil rather than as victims of a disease. Shockingly high numbers of them were imprisoned, tortured, and actually killed in order to exorcise the "demons" inhabiting their bodies.

We have come some distance since then in clarity and understanding, but we still have quite a way to go. Depression is now recognized by the medical profession as an illness that is significantly widespread to warrant professional attention, but the general public's knowledge of it is still alarmingly scant and often ill-informed.

Even doctors are still woefully ignorant of some of the illness's subtleties. If we knew as little about lung cancer, for example, as we do about depression, the disease would be responsible for many more smokers' lives than it currently claims.

Depression is nothing to be ashamed of, nothing to snigger about or guiltily conceal. It is an illness, like cancer or polio or asthma, from which numerous persons, both past and present, have suffered in needless silence. Such notable historical figures as Abraham Lincoln and Winston Churchill, for example, were apparently prey to the affliction. So familiar was Churchill with depression that he referred to it in his writing by a grim pet name—"my black dog," he called it.

Understanding the prevalence of depression can be a useful start toward recognizing its general symptoms. Today, this is more important than ever before. According to the National Institute of Mental Health, some 8,000,000 Americans each year suffer from a depression severe enough to warrant treatment. About 250,000 of these people receive hospital treatment for depression annually. Depression goes unrecognized in countless others, as evidenced by the high incidence of completed or attempted suicides, 70 to 80 percent of which are the result of depressive illness. Obviously, the time has long passed when we could afford to ignore the disturbance.

WHEN THE BLAHS BECOME THE BLUES

What does suicidal depression *feel* like? It's difficult for anyone who has never experienced it to comprehend the overwhelming, all-encompassing despair suffered by someone in the throes of a depression severe enough to make him or her want to stop living.

Of course, we have all experienced periods of discontent and uneasiness with our lives. "Gray," moody, or lackadaisical feelings are strangers to none of us. So common are such feelings, in fact, that our language has evolved a rich lexicon of slang expressions to describe them. We often speak of feeling "down" or "at wits' end," of having "gotten up on the wrong side of the bed," of feeling simply "blah."

But such feelings are so distinct in degree from what a seriously depressed person apparently feels as to constitute an entirely different cluster of emotions. Imagine the blahs becoming the blues, and the blues deciding to stay—not for an hour or a day, but for weeks, even months, so that it seems, finally, as if they will never end. You may then be able to appreciate the intensity of chronic depression, and understand why it sometimes drives its victims to despair and suicide.

Several years ago, a young actress wrote to me describing her feelings of depression. An attractive woman in her late thirties, Sallie first attempted suicide at the age of twelve and had made multiple suicide attempts by the time she first consulted me. She improved markedly with treatment and, at this point, sees me only when and if some crisis calls for additional counseling. Before treatment, however, she offered this vivid description of depression: "When you asked me how I feel when I'm suicidal, I could not really answer correctly at the time. You see, the pain and fear, the depression, the dread of not being able to cope, and feeling so horribly alone— fortunately, I forget these things when I feel fine. I remember them now because I am feeling them now.

"I want to run, to retreat. I feel such pressure and anger. I'm depressed and trapped. I feel I can't call anyone. I know from experience that they would try to understand, but that they cannot. And hearing 'Why don't you stop feeling sorry for yourself and straighten out?' only adds to my stress. If they only knew how I *want* to straighten out! It's hell to get these feelings. The fear of not getting out of a depression, of going into it deeper, is terrifying. A simple problem for them to solve is a tremendous problem for me.

"I really try. Sometimes I almost make it, but I seem to be like a child learning to walk—I keep falling down. I wonder if I'll ever stop falling. I feel so horribly alone that I can't talk to anyone and tell them how frightened I am, that at times I find life too overpowering for me, that I'm weak, and tired of trying to be strong."

This poignant description illustrates the chief aspects of chronic depression: fear, dread, anger, and an overwhelming sense of powerlessness. It also suggests one of the principal mistakes made by well-meaning friends and relatives who comprehend such depression only in terms of their own, relatively benign periods of feeling "blah." To demand of a severely depressed person, "Stop feeling sorry for yourself and snap out of it," makes very little sense from either a humane or a clinical standpoint. It's almost equivalent to demanding of a cancer patient that he or she "knock it off" and get back to work.

The first thing to remember about chronic or suicidal depression is that it is an affliction—an unwanted burden—which the person suffering it cannot simply take off like an old suit of clothes. Patience and therapy can cure the affliction; frustrated anger cannot.

But how can you tell when someone you know is severely depressed? How can you tell the blahs from the blues? This is not easy, but in the remainder of this chapter I will try to outline some of the more common signs or symptoms of severe depression, in the hope that they will enable you to recognize this increasingly common malaise.

SYMPTOMS OF DEPRESSION

Recognition of depression, even in its most extreme manifestations, can be difficult because the symptoms occur so commonly in everyday life that people minimize their significance or mislabel them.

The early signs, for example, tend to be temporary exaggerations of so-called normal experiences—mood swings, fatigue, loss of appetite or compulsive overeating, insomnia, early-morning wakening, an inability to concentrate, to name a few. And so they may go unnoticed or be explained away as insignificant. A loss of weight, for instance, may be attributed simply to a change of diet. Chronic fatigue may be attributed to "working too hard."

Physical symptoms often mask the presence of depression. An individual with headaches and insomnia may also experience fatigue, irritability, and an inability to concentrate at work. Attributing the depression to the persistent headaches and sleeplessness—and the resultant "inability to perform"— the individual may seek relief for the insomnia and headaches alone and not for the depression that is actually causing them.

Marital conflict, complicated by the loss of sexual drive and feelings of inadequacy, may also be mistakenly perceived as the cause of depression, rather than as the result of it. The same applies to appetite loss, compulsive overeating, gastric indigestion, constipation, backaches, stomachaches, and vague pains.

All of these can be physical manifestations of an underlying depression. Unfortunately, people suffering such symptoms generally choose to alleviate the symptoms and ignore the cause. Symptomatic relief thus becomes actually counterproductive. It is roughly comparable to giving the victim of a gunshot wound a painkiller: it relieves his immediate distress but does nothing about stopping the flow of blood.

The real cause of many physical ills, then, is emotional. This leads doctors to call such ills *psychosomatic,* indicating that they are induced mentally but manifested physically. This, in turn, leads many laypersons to view the ills as somehow less "real" or less painful than purely physical conditions.

This is a central error in the way we look at depressive symptoms.

It's crucial to remember that, except in a very few cases, depressed people are not merely "faking it." A psychosomatic headache can be every bit as painful, every bit as real, as one caused by migraine, eyestrain, or an excess of drink. It's inaccurate, therefore, to say that a disturbed person is merely imagining his or her discomfort. Depressed people genuinely experience their physical ailments. The power of the mind, even (or perhaps especially) the disturbed mind, is such that it can effect changes in the physical world; the headache that begins in a disordered brain, therefore, is felt eventually in the body. Not surprisingly, then, depressed people first seek treatment for the pain involved, rather than for the underlying depression.

When people suffer for considerable periods of time, their assorted symptoms can become an accepted part of their everyday lives, so that they don't look for help until they find it difficult or impossible to function. Even then, the depressed person may find outside "reasons" to blame for his or her distress. These rationalizations can sound quite plausible because the depressed person may indeed be under external stresses that would disturb anyone to some degree. It is the *degree* that determines the distinction between normal reactions to stress and the onset of depressive illness. What we need to measure is the duration and severity of the reaction. Symptoms that impair normal functioning beyond one or two weeks should be evaluated by the family physician. Even if objective external stresses exist, a dysfunction lasting this length of time suggests that help may be needed.

I want to look now at the more common symptoms of depression. All of these symptoms may of course be interpreted by the sufferer as well as by friends as nonproblematic. Yet a long duration of one or a group of them can indicate an underlying depression.

FATIGUE

Fatigue is one of the most common symptoms of depression. By fatigue I do not mean an occasional bout of exhaustion after a day's work, or the kind of purely physical anemia that is commonly, thanks to the Geritol company, known as "tired blood." Depressive fatigue is a condition of chronic listlessness which no amount of iron or vitamin supplements can remedy.

It varies, of course, from person to person. Some depressed individuals experience a sense of heaviness in the body and limbs; others, a loss of pep or energy. If you, or someone you know, complains of being "tired" all the time, and if body movements are noticeably slowed down, depression should be considered. It should also be considered as a possible affliction of people who find it difficult to concentrate or to maintain a sustained effort at their tasks. In its most acute form, depressive fatigue leads to feelings of apathy which can escalate into a crippling "paralysis of will" that allows the person to do little else but eat, watch TV, and sleep.

INSOMNIA

Insomnia, another common symptom of depression, has probably been experienced, at least in a mild form, by almost everyone at one time or another. In the past decade, much research has illuminated our knowledge of sleep. A normal night's sleep consists of four or five sleep cycles, each lasting about ninety minutes, and each consisting of four stages. The deepest stage is stage IV, or delta sleep, and the dream stage is stage I, or REM (rapid eye movement) sleep, so called because the eyes move in dreaming, as if we were watching our dreams.

Recent research has shown that although the amount of sleep needed nightly to maintain health varies considerably from person to person, a certain minimum of both REM and delta sleep is essential for both physical and mental well-being. Insufficient REM or delta sleep can result in disorientation, altered judgment, and/or lowered efficiency. Deprivation of REM sleep, which occurs in depression, can also result from use of alcohol and barbiturates and can lead to irritability and hallucinations.

Understanding the complexity of sleep and the constitutional factors that determine your sleep needs and patterns can be important. Some people who require only five or six hours of sleep a night, believing they need more, resort to sleeping pills or alcohol, not realizing that these drugs suppress REM sleep. Differences in the sleep patterns of a married couple can also create problems when one partner is a "night person" and the other is an "early-to-bed, early-to-rise" person.

The physician must look beyond sleep difficulties to the patient's age, general health (physical ailments can disrupt normal sleep patterns), family tensions, and other stresses. A disruption of sleep patterns is among the commonest evidence of underlying depression.

SEXUAL DISTURBANCES

Those who have studied the wide range of sexual practices throughout the world have observed that in sexual customs, as in customs of food preparation, there is little that is right or wrong, good or bad. Although attitudes toward specific sexual practices vary from one culture to the next, there is at least this constant: depression can play havoc with sexual performance.

Loss of libido (sexual drive), partial or complete impotence, and variations in the frequency of sexual activity ranging from inactivity to hyperactivity characterize sexual dysfunction in depression. Patients tend to complain of depression, however, only *after* they have noted a loss of libido. Thus, the depression is often attributed to the loss of libido—or to the interpersonal tensions produced by shifts in sexual patterns. Therefore, the underlying cause, the depression itself, may go untreated.

CHANGE IN APPETITE

The chronically depressed person may experience loss of interest in food, loss of taste for food, and finally loss of appetite, which may lead to significant weight loss. This is not to be confused with the unique syndrome of anorexia nervosa, which is characterized by radical weight loss, sometimes to the point of starvation and death, as well as by a variety of food fads and food phobias, and frequently follows in the wake of excessively vigorous efforts to lose weight.

While loss of appetite is a usual concomitant of depression, the opposite reaction also occurs.

It is perhaps not surprising that a person who feels himself or herself without options, spiritually or emotionally empty, should seek to offset that condition by eating. Cases of sudden obesity are common in the annals of depressive illness, as eating seems to provide a symbolic substitute for the emotional nourishment the depressed person really craves. The ironic tragedy of such substitution is that obesity is generally seen as one more piece of evidence of the depressed individual's worthlessness. Attempts to fill up an inner emptiness, then, by vigils before the refrigerator only lead to an intensification of the poor sense of self-esteem that led the depressed person to overeat in the first place.

Any radical change in eating habits should therefore be

viewed as evidence of a possible emotional disturbance. In cases of both overeating and undereating, the possibility of depression should be investigated.

PAIN

Pain frequently occurs in depression. It is difficult to pinpoint its link to an underlying depressive illness, however, unless all evidences of a physical disorder have been ruled out.

Such pain generally follows a pattern *previously experienced* by the depressed person. For example, someone whose arthritis has only occasionally flared up and caused pain might, when depressed, suffer intensified arthritic pain. Stress also lowers the pain threshold. The full pattern of responses to such pain includes sweating, dilation of pupils, reflex muscle spasms, and rapid heartbeat.

Anxiety accompanies the onset of pain in the average person. If the pain becomes chronic, it disrupts sleep, produces fatigue, reduces energy, and may lead to avoidance of sexual relations as well as work.

INABILITY TO WORK

In industry, declining performance and reduced drive are often treated as "morale" problems rather than as psychiatric disorders. Even when recognized, a depression may still not be treated as an illness, but be rationalized as "understandable" in terms of work stresses such as impending retirement, transfer, or even promotion.

Possible signs of work-related depression that are rarely recognized as symptoms include lateness, absenteeism, accident-proneness, diminished incentive, feelings of alienation, feelings of being worthless or unappreciated, inability to assume responsibility, inability to follow a routine, lack of assertiveness, diminished pride, and irritation with interference.

On the job, depressed individuals may find routine tasks burdensome and challenging tasks impossible. In the early stages of depression, a normally tense person may begin drinking more than the usual amount. A perfectionist will procrastinate. An impulsive person will make more than the usual quota of rapid-fire, off-the-cuff decisions.

Many depressed persons turn to the unmonitored use of stimulants, barbiturates, or tonics, which may lead to secondary complications more serious than the original symptoms. The individual's thinking may become so disturbed that he or she expresses ideas poorly or misunderstands the ideas of others. When this happens, performance suffers. Of course, poor performance may lead to the loss of one's job—in which case, the individual can cite a "good reason" for being depressed.

HYPOCHONDRIA

Hypochondria, or the feeling that one is constantly ill, may begin with a preoccupation with appearance, with aging, or with superficial body characteristics—the shape of the nose, breast, or ears, for instance, or the sagging of the skin, or the presence of a scar. While such fixations may not in and of themselves be abnormal, they should alert one to the possibility of depression—especially when some of the symptoms already discussed have also been noted.

This form of hypochondria can lead to a desire to alter one's appearance by drastic measures such as cosmetic surgery, face lifts, or hormone treatments. Such a concern reflects a morbid lowering of self-esteem. An improved sense of self-esteem usually returns after recovery from depression, but too many people go from one kind of treatment to another, searching for some magical change, then attribute their depression to the failure to be rejuvenated.

STRESS

Nobody lives without stress. The first day of school, examinations, a new job, a new neighborhood, illness—all can create stress. Even happy situations, such as marriage, the birth of a child, or the abundance of leisure after retirement, can create stress.

Although stress contributes to depression, it also is used to rationalize the presence of depression. Consider such common rationalizations as "Taxes are getting me down," "I'm worried about my kid making it to college," "Things have been getting a bit tense at home," or "My boss has it in for me."

To the extent that these and other pressures offer plausible explanations for mild to severe symptoms of depression, they tend to hide the need for professional help.

There are certain normal fluctuations of mood, thought, or behavior during stressful periods of life that can be mistakenly labeled as mental illness. However, psychological and behavioral changes during adolescence, the menopause, and old age are also often viewed as natural reactions, and the importance and feasibility of treatment are overlooked.

SENILITY

Psychiatric illness often goes undetected in the elderly because of the inclination to pass off aberrant moods or behavior as "senility" or simply "old age." This is particularly unfortunate considering the difficult situation in which old people today find themselves. Even the healthiest of our elderly no longer enjoy the traditional advantages of the extended family and small, close-knit communities, and their resulting isolation tends to intensify their feelings of loneliness and worthlessness. Symptoms of simply physical illness may be intensified by depression, as well as by the loss of the meaningful social roles that ordinarily make suffering more tolerable.

One of the interesting sidelights to depression among the elderly is that apparently it is often related to insomnia—a condition also common among the old. Deprived of that deep sleep from which younger people are hard to arouse by the progressive diminution of the delta phase of the sleep cycle with age, the elderly are particularly susceptible to early-morning daylight, room noises, and bodily urges, and therefore tend to sleep less than younger people. What is illuminating is that it has recently been shown that sleeplessness can contribute to the classic symptoms of senility, including forgetfulness and muddled thinking. In some cases, sedatives to ensure sleep have successfully reversed the mental deterioration, and thus the depression, of the old.

GETTING HELP

The loss of meaningful social roles and goals has affected many people. Modern society subjects people of all ages to enormous strains and stresses, while at the same time eliminating many of the activities and purposeful goals—involving family, church, and community—that once served to reduce stress and provide support.

The rapid rate of social change and the loss of traditional restraints, moreover, have reduced the stability of relationships and led to an increase in anxiety and depressive disorders, especially those associated with the fear of making bad choices. In addition, depressed people in our society often tend to blame circumstances or themselves for their depression. Family and friends tend to blame the symptoms on a lack of willpower or laziness. Tragically, the common insistence that the depressed person "apply himself" and "straighten out" only tends to deepen the sense of helplessness, worthlessness, and guilt.

Stopgap measures to obtain relief—such as tranquilizers, barbiturates, or over-the-counter sleeping aids—can be harmful in the long run. The only sure way to relieve depression is by getting professional help. If you or someone you know experiences the symptoms discussed in this chapter, you should consider such a course.

Remember that the "railroad track to hell" has many sidings—many opportunities to escape before the end of the line. One must first recognize the need for help, then seek it without shame. Depression *can* be treated.

3

Phase 1: Chemotherapy

Life was meant to be lived . . . one must never, for whatever reason, turn his back on life.
—ELEANOR ROOSEVELT

BREAKING THE CYCLE

Probably the most terrifying aspect of depression is the fact that, from the point of view of the person caught in it, it seems absolutely unalterable. The victim of depression, unlike the victim of most other diseases, is not blessed with the realization that the ailment will eventually pass and good health will return.

No matter how miserable the flu may make you feel, you know that if you can just grit your teeth for another day or another week, the sickness will lift and you will be able to resume your business again. The sufferer from chronic depression has no such hope. Caught in a vicious cycle of anxiety and hopelessness, he or she is in a position rather like that of the terminal cancer patient: all experience suggests to the sufferer that this will *never* end, short of death.

Imagine, then, that a person in such an apparently hopeless condition could be given a treatment that would very quickly indicate that things *could* be different, that the depressive cycle *could* be broken. You can well understand the euphoria, the sense of surprise and sudden possibility, that would envelop the person upon discovering that depression can be wiped away.

This is the purpose of chemotherapy.

The use of antidepressant and other mood-elevating drugs under proper medical supervision can literally open up new vistas to the chronically depressed person. It can give him or her the necessary boost that the angry or frustrated exhortations of friends are powerless to give. It can boost the person up to peer in timid wonder over a wall. It can alleviate all symptoms in a matter of weeks or at least in sufficient degree to enable him or her to start living again.

Now, drugs alone are not the complete answer. As potent a force for change as chemotherapy is, I hasten to add that usually it is only the first step in an ongoing process of rehabilitation, a phase I that can get things moving by breaking the self-destructive cycle. While many patients are restored to normal functioning with drugs alone, the majority of depressed patients need the complement of phase II, psychotherapy, to reach full recovery and evolve more sensible strategies for daily living so as to prevent repeated episodes.

Consider, for example, the case of Frank, a young commercial artist who, when he walked into our clinic eight years ago, had just unsuccessfully attempted suicide.

At the age of thirty-two, practically everything Frank had tried to do with his life had failed: his marriage, a subsequent relationship, his career as a commercial artist, even his attempt to take his life.

Everything about him—from his droopy posture and lackluster clothing to his limp handshake and nonassertive manner—betrayed his low opinion of himself. He looked and acted like the proverbial "loser."

At the advertising agency where he worked, Frank was a member of the "bullpen," one of the lowest positions in the art department. There he did lettering and paste-ups on ads created by staff art directors. Although he had been working there for years, this menial position seemed to him the end of the line.

Frank now works as a vice-president of a large advertising agency in the Midwest and is considered one of the top art directors in his field. He exudes the confident, aggressive manner of a man accustomed to assuming responsibility. And rightly so, for advertising agencies and their clients don't entrust television commercials with million-dollar budgets to a loser.

What happened in the intervening years to turn this loser into a winner?

Treatment, of course; but first, chemotherapy. My initial efforts focused on helping Frank to change a vicious cycle of ineffectual patterns of daily living, which produced anxiety and in turn intensified his ineffectual life patterns.

Anxious about his many failures, Frank marked time in his job, fearing further catastrophes, and this only ensured that he would stay right where he was—as an unassertive, timid, walking failure. His behavior recalled British therapist R. D. Laing's description of a self-destructive life cycle in his book of poetry, *Knots:*

> I am not entitled to what I have
> *therefore* everything I have is stolen.
> If I've got it,
> and I am not entitled to it,
> I *must* have stolen it,
> *because* I am not entitled to it.

How do you begin to break such a self-demeaning cycle? In Frank's case, as in many others, we begin by reducing anxieties as quickly as possible with chemotherapy.

In the past two decades, powerful antidepressant medicines have been discovered that relieve much of the distress of depression rapidly and economically. In addition, the psycho-pharmaceuticals (also called psychotropic drugs) quickly free the depressed and suicidal person from obsessive thoughts of guilt, self-doubt, self-hate, and hypochondriacal fears. In this chapter I will describe some of the common drugs used in chemotherapy and try to answer the more common questions people raise about their use.

Why do these drugs work?

Numerous studies have linked depressive symptoms to physiological and biochemical changes in the nervous system involving certain brain hormones and enzymes. The precise pattern of cause and effect remains undetermined, but it is clear that chemistry can alter our mood, disposition, and behavior. It may be that stress produces chemical changes in the brain that lead to altered behavior. Or it may be that stress simply throws a fragile, chemically imbalanced nervous system further off balance.

In any event, what the psychopharmaceutical drugs do is restore the brain enzymes and hormones to normal functioning. This restoration of chemical balance can reduce a broad range of symptoms from a dangerously suicidal to a normal state.

Do the drugs cure?

Psychopharmaceuticals don't cure in and of themselves. But they do have significant and predictable effects which reduce or eliminate the symptoms of depression. This, in turn, gives the individual a positive, hopeful attitude toward the *possibility* of personal change.

Relieved of symptoms and restored to a normal emotional state, the individual can look at problems more objectively, so that what appeared to be insurmountable difficulties at home, on the job, or in personal relationships start to appear manageable or reduced to one or two problem areas.

Please remember that the use of chemotherapy does not in

any way minimize the importance of phase II of treatment: psychotherapy. Drugs are an important beginning, but only a beginning.

Now, how do these drugs work?

ANTIDEPRESSANTS

The two major classes of antidepressants, tricyclic agents and monoamine oxidase (MAO) inhibitors, both tend to improve your motivation, energy, sleep, appetite, and concentration. They also help to dispel the marked emptiness and inertia that severely depressed patients often describe. Nevertheless, they differ in several important ways.

TRICYCLIC AGENTS

The first drug a doctor will generally prescribe for a depressed patient is one of the tricyclics. These include such drugs as amitriptyline (Elavil), doxepin (Sinequan), desipramine (Norpramin), imipramine (Tofranil), protriptyline (Vivactil), perphenazine-amitriptyline (Etrafon, Triavil), and chlordiazepoxide-amitriptyline (Limbitrol). They work by preventing the breakdown of serotonin, norepinephrine, and dopamine, the so-called mood-normalizing brain hormones involved in depression.

Tricyclics usually require two or three weeks to take effect. Even then, the first signs may be temporary and limited to one or two symptoms only. In fact, improvement may zigzag, with good periods followed by a fleeting return of symptoms. However, the odds are that once improvement begins, overall progress will continue and there will be relief of the remaining symptoms.

If after several weeks on one or more of the tricyclics, at

maximum dosage, no response has occurred, an MAO inhibitor will be tried.

MONOAMINE OXIDASE INHIBITORS

As the name suggests, MAO inhibitors inhibit the action of monoamine oxidase (MAO), an enzyme. MAO produces depression by breaking down the natural stimulant norepinephrine, a hormone that plays an important role in the transmission of nerve impulses.

The MAO inhibitors include such drugs as phenelzine sulfate (Nardil), tranylcypromine (Parnate), and isocarboxazid (Marplan).

If your doctor prescribes an MAO inhibitor, he or she will monitor your progress carefully, especially for signs of low blood pressure, such as lightheadedness or dizziness. Such effects can easily be controlled by adjusting your medication.

You should know that certain foods and medicines must be avoided if you're on MAO inhibitors. Of particular danger are chicken liver, aged cheese, pickled herring, alcohol, and medicines containing epinephrine—including novocaine and nasal sprays. These produce enzymes that can interact with the MAO inhibitors, producing serious hypertensive crises.

WHAT ABOUT SIDE EFFECTS?

Almost any drug involves the risk of some side effects during the initial stages of treatment. With either group of antidepressants, perspiration, dry mouth, constipation, slugglishness, blurred vision, and dizziness may occur. Generally such side effects are only temporary and need not be cause for concern. If they persist, contact your physician.

Occasionally, antidepressants induce a state of elation or excitement. This can be controlled by reducing the dosage.

HOW LONG MUST ONE TAKE ANTIDEPRESSANTS?

In most instances, I prescribe a full dose for three to six months, and then a maintenance dosage for several months more. Most depressions lift within this time. Some patients may require medication for longer periods. Frank, who is no longer in active treatment, nevertheless continues on medication as an extra measure of security. This gives him the courage to live his life in ways that maximize his potential.

Unfortunately, doctors cannot yet predict which patients will need long-term antidepressants and which will not. Remember that it takes ten days to three weeks for most antidepressant medicines to reach effective levels in the body. So if you should begin taking an antidepressant, don't be discouraged if you don't respond right away. And *don't stop taking the medicine.* Give it a chance to work.

TRANQUILIZERS

Tranquilizers are used to treat anxiety, tension, and agitation, all of which often occur in depression.

You probably have your personal definition of anxiety. Some people describe a sinking feeling in the pit of the stomach, or a heart that won't stop racing, thoughts they can't turn off, a tightness in the chest, or shortness of breath.

Doctors define this condition as an alarm state characterized by apprehensive, excessive alertness, sweating palms, rapid heartbeat and breathing, dilated pupils, and high blood pressure. Some individuals find it an exciting state, but most find it unnerving, since an excess of excitement can overwhelm and incapacitate a person. At its worst, such a condition can paralyze the will and initiate a cycle of defensive behavior that only intensifies the anxiety.

Tranquilizers such as Valium, Librium, Serax, Tranxene, and others commonly prescribed can break the cycle of anxiety by easing symptoms. However, people suffering such anxiety "attacks" may also be helped to realize that anxiety is generally limited in time and triggered by specific situations. If you are a victim of this kind of condition, you should know that in addition to drugs there are several techniques that others have found helpful in reducing anxiety—among them biofeedback and autogenic training, as well as many meditational techniques.

BARBITURATES

I spoke earlier of the predominance of insomnia in depression. Insomnia, however, is a broader problem than depressive illness; many nondepressed persons suffer from it, too. So common is the inability to sleep, in fact, that it has been estimated that one out of every six adult Americans uses or has used some type of sleeping pill at one time or another.

Barbiturates (Seconal, Phenobarbital, and Nembutal) are the most frequently prescribed sedatives. Like another category of sedatives, the hypnotics (which don't hypnotize, but make you drowsy), *barbiturates can be dangerous.* While they alleviate insomnia rapidly, reliably, and effectively, they can produce problems of tolerance and addiction. Users of barbiturates should be aware, for example, that prolonged use leads to a condition of tolerance characterized by the need for increased dosages to produce *equivalent, or even reduced, effects.*

Some barbiturates lose their effectiveness within weeks, leading to a condition known as *drug-dependency insomnia.* In one study, a group of long-term barbiturate users who continued to receive their usual sedatives ended up sleeping as poorly as, or worse than, a comparable group of insomniacs who received no medication at all!

In addition, barbiturates frequently create what is called a *psychological dependence:* even if the body is not habituated to the pills, the insomniac may become so used to having them that he or she firmly believes that it is impossible to sleep without them.

But this is not the most serious problem associated with barbiturates. Habitual sleeping-pill users, it is believed, suffer the suppression of REM sleep—and this, as noted in Chapter 2, can have a harmful, disorienting effect. In some cases, failure to get enough REM sleep can lead to hallucinations. In addition, the indiscriminate use of sleeping pills can easily delude an insomniac into believing that their effectiveness in inducing sleep is actually a cure for the condition—while the underlying causes of sleeplessness go uninvestigated. Finally, hypnotics—even the supposedly benign varieties sold over the counter—can lead to actual habituation, poisoning, and death. Among the drugs listed as potentially habit-forming by the Federal Drug Administration, for example, is scopolamine, an ingredient of some sleep aids such as Sleep-Eze, Sominex, and Sure-Sleep.

BARBITURATE ADDICTION

Excessive and prolonged use of barbiturates can lead to addiction characterized by severe withdrawal symptoms lasting up to twelve months after cessation of drug use. The late novelist Evelyn Waugh ran out of his "sleepers" aboard a ship to Ceylon in 1954. As reported in the *British Medical Journal,* he developed hallucinations and thought he was diabolically possessed. The hallucinations persisted for weeks, clearing up only gradually with treatment. Physical dependency on sleeping pills is very easy to establish and very hard to reverse.

BARBITURATE POISONING

If you don't fall asleep after the first or second dose of a sleeping pill, you may unwittingly take an overdose. Afterward, upon recovering, you will probably have no memory of taking the additional doses. In addition, it is unfortunately not at all difficult to take a *fatal* overdose of these pills.

You've undoubtedly seen countless headlines announcing that such-and-such a celebrity was "found dead of an overdose." The story usually goes on to say that the overdose was "accidental." Maybe so. Cases of accidental barbiturate poisoning are common. Moreover, as the tragic case of Karen Ann Quinlan has shown, many people suffer the fatal or near-fatal consequences of mixing alcohol and barbiturates—a deadly combination. In addition, many overdoses are intentional. To compound the danger, barbiturates, which are supposed to relieve the symptom of insomnia, sometimes *produce* other depressive symptoms that in turn can prompt a suicide attempt.

STIMULANTS

In mild depressions, stimulants such as dexedrine and amphetamines generally alleviate loss of energy and interest. In most cases, however, stimulants, commonly known as "pep pills" or "speed," merely supplement the antidepressants. *The indiscriminate use of stimulants can produce psychosis.* They can also produce feelings of "energy" and alertness in someone who is actually tired and needs rest. This is particularly dangerous when one is operating a car, a motorcycle, or heavy equipment.

You can also build up a tolerance to stimulants that, as with barbiturates, can lead to increased dosage and the danger of toxicity. Even more dangerous, a seriously depressed or suicidal person could be energized enough by stimulants to *attempt* suicide. Finally, an "energy letdown" often occurs when tolerance sets in or the drug is discontinued, and this can cause a depressed person to become even *more* depressed.

Such a letdown used to be known, in the 1960s, as the "crash" after a "high." It would be well to remember in this regard that by the end of that drug-happy decade, even heavy users of hallucinogens and other psychotropic drugs were warning that stimulants were tricky and should probably be avoided. In the street cliché of the time, "Speed kills."

LITHIUM

So far, I have been talking about drugs that are designed to combat some of the symptoms of the classic, one-way depression. There is, however, a special variety of depression that has recently received much public attention, and it is for this type of depression that the widely available drug lithium is generally prescribed.

I am speaking of the swinging-pendulum variety of depression, which all of us experience in mild forms as a shifting of moods from happy to glum and back again. John Milton, in his *Paradise Lost*, spoke of it as "demoniac frenzy, moping melancholy." Traditionally, doctors have referred to it as *manic-depression*, or *bipolar depression*. In the popular literature today, the less forbidding term *mood swing* is often employed.

With the availability of treatment for the condition, more cases are being recognized than ever before. Recently, a famous director traveled the TV talk-show circuit to describe how lithium carbonate has controlled his manic-depressive episodes. Popular magazines have heralded the "new miracle drug." Two episodes of the TV situation comedy "Maude" were devoted to the heroine's oscillation between frenzied, extravagant activity (running up a $1,600 phone bill, tossing $50 tips around) and deep depression ("I did everything wrong"). Diagnosed as manic-depressive, she received lithium therapy and recovered.

Lithium has been known for centuries. The ancient Greeks, according to Hippocrates, used mineral spring waters containing lithium salts to treat "mania" and "melancholy." Bottled spring waters such as Vichy and Perrier also contain lithium and have been sold for their "curative" properties.

Lithium works by stabilizing moods that swing periodically between elation and despair—the condition known as bipolar depression. In addition, lithium has been effective with unipolar (recurrent) depressions, which lack the dramatic mood swings of manic-depression. It won't stop one's current bout of depression, but it could prevent the next one.

Essentially, lithium works for patients whose recurrent depressions have occurred periodically or cyclically, independent of their life circumstances. Such patients sometimes become depressed even when their life situation is satisfactory. The manic periods, as noted, have often been attributed erroneously to a "sense of relief" from the depression, when in fact they represent a clue to the existence of an underlying bipolar depression. The signs of the upward mood swings may blend with normal reactions and may not be recognized. In most people, the upward mood swing masquerades as relief. "Gosh, I feel great now that I'm no longer depressed," you tell yourself, when in fact relief has a slightly manic (hypomanic) tinge to it.

How can you recognize a bipolar depression? Be alert to the following:

1. *Short-lived bursts of enormous energy.* The individual demonstrates alertness, activity, and creativity in developing ideas. He or she may become the "life of the party," even when gaiety is inappropriate to the situation.

2. **Enormous self-confidence.** In the manic phase, the individual has little self-doubt and a tremendous capacity for influencing people and events.

3. **Overtalkativeness.** The individual may appear overactive, overconfident, and unable to be silent. He or she appears to be inexhaustible, forever radiating an infectious vigor and enthusiasm. During "high" periods, manic-depressives accomplish much of the work they could not do during the low or depressed phase.

The manic pole can therefore seem quite attractive. But it has a negative dimension. Manic individuals may be impatient, frustrated, intolerant of others, and impulsive. They may foolishly rush into business deals or make commitments beyond their capacity to fulfill. They may unnecessarily expose themselves to danger. Easily bored and distracted, they may engage in a flurry of miscellaneous projects that they never complete.

Excessive expenditure of energy may lead to grandiose delusions of power, hypersensitivity, and then exhaustion, which can be frightening both for the individual and for those around him or her.

Fortunately, lithium can control these symptoms. It may also prove valuable in the treatment of premenstrual tension, phobic anxiety, obsessional neurosis, schizophrenia, and alcohol addiction, but conclusive evidence for this has not yet been presented.

SIDE EFFECTS OF LITHIUM

There are a number of side effects associated with high doses of lithium. It may cause dry mouth, shakiness, and jitteriness, which should be brought to the physician's attention. Regular blood tests should be taken in the early stages of lithium treatment, then every six months thereafter, as long as treatment continues. The possibility of toxic reactions from very high doses and/or from the body's failure to excrete lithium prohibits its use in patients suffering from kidney or cardiovascular disease.

HOW LONG ON LITHIUM?

As yet, no one knows how long a patient must remain on lithium. Numerous patients have taken it for close to fifteen years with considerable success. Cost is not a prohibitive factor because availability of lithium in nature has made it relatively inexpensive.

GUIDELINE FOR TAKING DRUGS

Antidepressants, tranquilizers, and lithium do not produce addiction. Yet some patients express fear of addiction and refuse to take them. Others refuse medication for religious reasons. One elderly woman patient of mine had a succession of depressive illnesses during her late sixties and early seventies. Because of her religious beliefs, Anna refused medication until she had become so disturbed that she could not function. When she came to my clinic, she was on the verge of suicide.

Fortunately, I was able to work around Anna's resistance and help her to come to terms with the need for chemotherapy. She began to take her medication willingly. But when she began to feel better, she stopped taking the medication, with the result that she became depressed and suicidal again.

This story has a happy ending, as well as an important lesson to impart.

The recurrence of Anna's illness convinced her of *the need to follow instructions,* despite her reservations about taking drugs. Today, in spite of her years, she is working part-time as a legal secretary and functioning well.

I think Anna's case is interesting because her treatment was very much dependent upon the maintenance of her medication. Here the whole art of chemotherapy came into play. That art includes the importance of choosing the right medication as well as the need for a supportive and sympathetic attitude toward the patient.

HOSPITALIZATION

Chemotherapy has dramatically reduced the need to hospitalize patients.

If required, hospitalization usually takes place during the initial stages of treatment, when symptoms are most intense. New crises or a recurrence of symptoms severe enough to produce disturbed behavior—a strong feeling of losing control, for instance—may indicate the advisability of brief rehospitalization. Generally, however, patients on chemotherapy simply do not require the constant supervision a hospital affords.

SHOCK THERAPY OR CHEMOTHERAPY?

Controversy regarding its efficacy and safety still surrounds the use of electroconvulsive shock therapy (ECT), or the administration of electric shock (usually 150 to 170 volts) to the brain. Many physicians have found less need to rely upon ECT since the advent of chemotherapy, and restrict its use to hospitalized patients who don't respond to medicine or remain severely agitated. Shock therapy often works more rapidly than chemotherapy in alleviating symptoms, but it may impair memory and cause confusion. Moreover, ECT does not prevent *recurrent* episodes. Generally speaking, chemotherapy has been found to be more predictable and more easily administered, and so is more widely applicable than shock therapy.

I recall a patient whose case illustrates the changing experience of chronic illness with the advent of new therapeutic modalities.

Molly, a woman in her sixties, had been given shock treatments once or twice a year for fifteen years because of depressions. Every time she traveled abroad, she had to be hospitalized for depression.

A fearful, emotional woman who came to the United States in the 1930s as a refugee from Nazism, she responded poorly to stress. She would either go into a depression or be off on a manic shopping spree.

Today, Molly is fine. For the past seven years, she has been on lithium maintenance, visiting my office only twice a year for a blood test. She no longer suffers from manic or depressive episodes, and no longer requires shock therapy or hospitalization. For the last five years, Molly has visited her children and grandchildren abroad without a qualm.

FROM PHASE 1 TO PHASE 2

Prediction of the exact pattern of improvement on medication can be difficult because of the numerous factors involved.

The pattern and progress of treatment may fluctuate because of the severity of the illness, the objective stresses in the patient's life, the patient's confidence in the therapist, and his or her expectations about the treatment and medication prescribed.

The fastest recovery, of course, occurs when the *specific* stresses precipitating the depression have been eliminated.

But however rapid or slow the progress on chemotherapy, one thing should always be kept in mind. The use of mood-altering drugs, while an essential and valuable aspect of treatment, must be seen as only the first step in an entire program of treatment. Drugs can alleviate immediate stress quite effectively, but they cannot tackle the underlying emotional disorder that both creates the life situations that produce stress for the patient and makes that stress so debilitating for the suicidally depressed person. That is the task of phase II of treatment: psychotherapy.

In the following two chapters I will discuss the deeper emotional problems involved in depression, show how they come about, and explain how psychotherapy is designed to deal with them.

4

Causes of Depression

In my end is my beginning.
—T. S. Eliot, *East Coker*

Why is it that two people born into the same family, subject to virtually the same early childhood experiences, can turn out so differently—one developing a psychiatric disorder, the other not?

Early life experiences do shape your basic personality. Whether or not you develop a psychiatric illness, however, is related to a complex host of factors—inherited biological and constitutional factors as well as early experiences. Some depressive conditions may even have a genetic basis. This doesn't mean that a person with a particular genetic makeup is fated to act in a designated manner later in life, but it does mean that he or she may be *predisposed* to certain kinds of reactions, moods, and behavior.

In addition, we are all, to some extent, predisposed to psychological disorder, inasmuch as we all carry within us the seeds of imbalance as well as those of health. Given that we may all be prone to illness, both physical and mental, we may say that depression or other psychological disorders may occur at that point where social and/or personal stresses impinge upon our particular constitution in such a way as to impair our ability to function. These social and personal stresses do not *cause* depression per se, but they act to trigger, perpetuate, and aggravate it.

In this chapter we will examine some of the ways in which the rise of depression has been explained, and we will be looking at theories that concentrate on both the personal and the social causes of the disorder.

PSYCHOANALYTIC PERSPECTIVES

The early psychoanalysts focused on the similarity of depressive illness to the grief of mourning. Freud emphasized the psychological importance of a subjective sense of loss—the loss of a loved one or the loss of self-esteem.

According to psychoanalytic theory, the guilt and self-accusation so common among depressed patients mask feelings of anger and hostility toward a lost love object. Because the individual experiences guilt over feeling anger toward loved ones, and therefore has difficulty in expressing that anger, he or she internalizes and directs it toward himself or herself.

The lost love object may be anyone from a spouse to a parent, child, or friend whom the depressed person perceives as having betrayed him or her by leaving. Often, but not always, the lost beloved leaves by dying. Sometimes he or she may have withdrawn—or threatened to withdraw—affection.

Thus, Freud conceived of depression as an unconscious reaction to a *real or imagined loss* of a love object (who is therefore both loved and hated). Melanie Klein, a neo–Freudian therapist, linked depression to early infancy, when the infant first reacts to decreasing maternal support with anger, and then with guilt. In addition, the depressed person may have learned in childhood to anticipate the parents' punishment, and inwardly punished himself or herself after committing some infraction of their rules. Children who were especially sensitive to parental criticism can turn into adults who are still seeking to avoid that criticism, who are morbidly fearful of a loss of love or esteem.

While all of us are dependent on our past to some extent, seriously depressed individuals feel that dependency as helplessness, sometimes to the point of regressing to infantile behavior patterns such as sucking their thumbs or refusing to eat. Tragically, such behaviors restore them to exactly the condition of powerlessness they most fear.

Since everyone experiences some disappointment in the process of growing up, everyone carries some residual inclination to depression and withdrawal. The birth of a sibling might have seemed to take parental attention, for example. Other demands on parents might have reduced their free time and increased their irritability. Without loving reassurances, feelings of hopelessness and self-blame may have become habitual for the child. Children raised in emotionally nonsupportive orphanages, for instance, have higher rates of illness, death, and depression than children raised in supportive orphanages.

A vast array of past conditioning experiences contributes to the way in which each person functions. With maturity, many people increase their self-awareness and their capacity to anticipate and protect themselves from difficult situations. Nevertheless, they may still respond to stressful events with the same automatic defenses they used in the past. And defensiveness, in turn, evokes responses in others that create more stress, further jarring the individual's sensitivities and increasing the likelihood of depressive reactions.

ROOTS OF DEPENDENCY

Culture constitutes one of the most powerful forces that shape our lives. From the great number of universal responses of which infants and children are capable, each culture selectively reinforces certain characteristic attitudes and behavior patterns, and these then tend to become typical of the specific culture.

The British, for example, are said to be more reserved than Americans, perhaps because life on a crowded island is pleasanter if one adheres to a strict sense of social distinction, along with a respect for privacy. Arabs, on the other hand, seem to enjoy crowding together. Their normal conversational distance (about thirteen to fourteen inches apart) is roughly half that of Americans and Britons.

Cultural factors, mediated through parents and family, influence our emotional responses, our interpersonal relationships, and our characteristic ways of coping with stress. In time, these patterns evolve into our *personality*, a system of defenses or adaptive mechanisms that assist us in coping with daily life.

However crucial culture may be in determining our response to the world, it can hardly be considered more important than the training one receives at the hands of one's earliest teachers and transmitters of mores: one's parents and siblings. Under their guidance, we receive a set of core attitudes and behavioral options that we carry with us throughout our later experiences. This cannot be emphasized too much. Each stage of your childhood training—when you learned to walk, talk, control your bowels, and the like—has some component that subsequently influences your attitudes and behavior.

The most crucial period of this training occurs during the initial stages of infancy. It is a time of total dependency, a time when an infant is helpless and incapable of functioning without the support of others. It is a time when either too much or too little gratification can influence adult dependent behavior.

Excessive gratification of the infant's needs at this stage may foster an overly optimistic view of the world. When translated into adult behavior, this may result in an inclination to expect others to please him, and a need to make extra efforts to get them to do so. The fully gratified child has the possibility of developing into an adult who thinks the world "owes him a living."

If at a later stage of infancy, when an overly gratified child has gained some mastery over the world, his needs are then frustrated, feelings of abandonment may result. This may lead to a personality marked both by smug confidence and a tendency to be critical and rejecting of others.

Punishment of dependent behavior at a still later stage may lead to the persistence of the dependent behavior because it produces feelings of worthlessness and an acute sensitivity to rejection, and this sense of worthlessness, paradoxically, may have become more familiar, and thus more acceptable, to the person than healthier feelings of self-esteem. Often the person who has been excessively dependent as a child finds later that he or she is unable to tap inner resources, since they have been so long unused that they have shriveled through neglect. This, not surprisingly, can lead to a sense of despair and uselessness.

To some extent, this is a basic problem in the growth and development of *all* people because everyone goes through a certain amount of frustration in the process of growing up. At some time or other, each of us has experienced someone withdrawing from us. We respond to these frustrations differently, however. Chronically depressed people generally are more gravely victimized by dependency than others. Their responses to frustration include the following patterns:

1. They continually seek approval and support, constantly testing the responsiveness of others, so that they are, in effect, continually "asking" to be hurt.

2. They lean on others to the point where others are forced to reject them.

3. They are afraid to do independently what is likely to give them a positive sense of self because of an excessive need for approval from others.

4. They rarely experience feelings of satisfaction from their own accomplishments.

5. Occasionally, they rely excessively on charm to ingratiate themselves with others.

This sort of behavior stems from an unmet need persisting from childhood to be accepted and to gain the love and approval of others. The more these needs govern your behavior, the less sure of yourself you will be, and the more prone to depression.

Some chronically depressed people sometimes act in a grandiose, omnipotent way, becoming so exhilarated and euphoric that they overcommit themselves to some task or project. Then, feeling overwhelmed, they find themselves retreating, unwilling to assume responsibility. Often their grandiosity fluctuates with periods when they feel empty and unable to recognize and accept offers of genuine concern from others. As you will recognize from the description in Chapter 3, such behavior is typical of bipolar depression.

Cyclical mood swings originate, in part, in childhood—that is, to the degree to which parents set limits on exuberance. When parents who place great emphasis on achievement also encourage the containment of feelings, an explosive situation sometimes results. When the message to the child is "Calm down—it's bad to show emotion," the child feels frustrated and resentful. As these resentful, unallowable feelings accumulate, so does the need to get out of this uncomfortable state until eventually the child swings to the other extreme, the "high" of euphoria.

Some children come to rely on these highs for feelings of self-worth. Later in life, during periods of depression, they yearn to be childishly exuberant again, partly as a way to compensate for feeling low. This, too, is a form of dependency. It becomes the therapist's task in such cases to assist the individual to accept himself or herself in a relatively normal state, not just in a euphoric one.

STILL THE ANGRY CHILD

The more severe types of depressive illness are generally the result of a strong predisposition to psychosis coupled with an early family situation that unreasonably both punishes and aggravates dependency. For example, children who must contend with the demands of overcritical or brutal parents sometimes never develop the ability to deal realistically with the adult world. Living for years in a threatening environment of exalted standards and harsh recrimination, an environment moreover in which anger cannot be adequately acknowledged or expressed for fear of reprisals, such individuals learn to accept as "normal" a state of continual unresolved conflict. They are forever torn between feelings of suspiciousness and feelings of dependency. This creates a dilemma: How can you accept support from others when you don't feel you can trust them to provide it? How can you communicate with others when your earliest training suggests they are all out to "get" you?

This constitutes a terrible, self-defeating cycle. The individual struggles to obtain the support he or she needs but never expects to receive. Uncertainty pushes the individual to test the people in his or her environment—that is, to try to *elicit* rejection to see if in fact it exists. As a result, because of negative expectations, the individual often gets exactly what he or she expects: rejection. And the more the person focuses on the struggle, the more he or she suppresses the positive, creative aspects of the personality.

I recall one such patient, Brian, who had a life history of suicide attempts. Brian's childhood had been disastrous. He had an alcoholic father who beat his son for the slightest "infraction" and also abused his frantic, insecure wife. Abused by her husband, Brian's mother also took out her frustrations on the boy.

In this atmosphere of constant vindictiveness and rejection, Brian grew hypersensitive to even imagined rejection. Feeling unloved and unwanted, he defensively carried a chip on his shoulder. Whenever people did anything nice for him, he didn't trust them, but had to test them, prod them, challenge them until they (as he had convinced himself they would) rejected him. In this way, he again and again confirmed the notion, driven into him by his childhood experiences, that he was unworthy of people's love.

Eventually Brian sought therapy. But tragically, he did so too late. Like so many others suffering from severe suicidal depressions, he was too ashamed to seek professional help at a time when that help might have turned his life around. When he did come, it was not so much as a patient seeking medical assistance as a still-angry child, expecting to find in the authority figure of the therapist the same critical abuse that had been heaped on him for so many years.

Instead, he found acceptance and something he had never encountered before: progress. Ironically, this created more of a conflict than his battered psyche could withstand; he could not let himself believe that he was not once again failing to live up to his unreasonably high standards of behavior. In spite of the gains he had made, at the age of twenty-eight he took his revenge on a world that had consistently abused him, by jumping in front of a train and ending his life.

Fortunately, the Brians of this world are a scant minority. But even that minority could be helped if only they sought assistance for their depressions *early* enough, and stuck with treatment *long* enough for it to show results.

Psychotherapy, following on chemotherapy, has been shown to be an effective method of dealing with countless cases of suicidal depression. Sadly, there will always be a few Brians who cannot be reached by these methods, whose childhood scars are too deep to permit access by either drugs or counseling. For most of us still-angry children, however, the combination of the two methods has worked, and will continue to work.

In the following chapter I will discuss specifically how phase II of a program of treatment can help suicidally depressive patients to avoid Brian's unhappy fate.

5

Phase 2: Psychotherapy

If I am not for myself, who will be for me? If I am for
myself alone, what am I? If not now, when?
—HILLEL, *Ethics of the Fathers*

WHAT IS PSYCHOTHERAPY?

Let's say that, after a long period of depression, you decide
that suicide is beginning to look too close for comfort, and you
seek professional help. Your therapist starts you at once on
antidepressant medication, and to your delight you begin to
feel better for the first time in years. You stop moping around,
you stop berating yourself for your failings, and you find
yourself able to work with greater gusto and enjoyment.

But something is missing.

In spite of the fact that your life seems to be picking up,
there are still numerous questions for which you have no
answers. You know that you've been chronically depressed,
but not why. And you've been made aware by your therapist
that although the medication you are taking can deal almost
indefinitely with the symptoms of your ailment, that ailment
can be finally eradicated only by a process of investigation and
understanding that you yourself must initiate. Drugs, you

realize, are not enough; you must begin to see why the drugs were needed in the first place.

It is time for you to enter phase II of treatment: psychotherapy.

Psychotherapy today, whether of the Freudian, Gestalt, or any of a number of eclectic varieties, has proved itself a valuable weapon in the attack on countless chronically depressed persons' illnesses. With the advent of public therapy clinics, moreover, a method of treatment that used to be the prerogative of the wealthy alone has become available to people of more modest means, so that today more people are regularly seeking therapy than ever before.

In spite of the popularity of the method, however, psychotherapy is still shrouded in a great deal of mumbo-jumbo and mystery. Four decades after Freud's death, the dominant public image of the "shrink" is that of a bearded patriarch with heavy spectacles who sits solemnly in judgment at the head of a couch, making cryptic notes on a pad and shouting "Aha!" whenever the patient mentions the words "bathroom" or "mother."

This image does a disservice to therapists, and it is not suprising that with such a forbidding notion in mind many people who could benefit from the method are instead frightened away by it. The prospect of putting yourself in the hands of a brooding authoritarian figure who "knows something you don't" is understandably intimidating to people who are already wary of criticism and rejection. I sometimes think the cause of therapy—and thus of public health—would be best served if all therapists were required to swear, upon entering practice, to wear only loud sports jackets and to guffaw at least once an hour.

Psychotherapists, like any other class of people, are just that: people. They are not divinely inspired gurus or calculating computers of emotional ledger sheets, but merely professional men and women who perform for disordered minds the same kind of service that general physicians perform for the body.

Ideally, their task is not to trip you up, or to fix blame, or to make you do anything you don't want to do. What they are supposed to do is help you get back on your own best track by enabling you to see things you cannot or are reluctant to look at alone.

What can you expect from therapy?

First of all, you *cannot* expect the therapist to hand you a neat outline of all your problems, with prescriptions to remedy each one. As the therapist Hannah Green put it in her moving novel, "I never promised you a rose garden." The job of the therapist is to assist you in learning to make your own decisions, solve your own problems, be your own person.

I spoke in the last chapter about how dependency patterns inherited from childhood very often imprison the adult, making him or her a victim of memories and expectations long beyond his or her control. In the simplest sense, the primary task of the therapist is to release the patient from these patterns, to open the prison—or, more accurately, *to show the patient how to open it.*

As for the actual process of psychotherapy, a great deal of mystification has clouded that issue as well. People unfamiliar with the actual processes speak of "transference" and "the dynamics of interaction," of "free association" and "breakthroughs," as if they were parts of an arcane ritual to which only a few elect are granted admittance.

In fact, therapy is an opportunity to get a better handle on your problems, with the therapist providing a sympathetic ear, an informed awareness of the human mind, and an occasional verbal prod to get the patient looking in the right direction.

THE THREE TASKS OF THERAPY

Above all else, psychotherapy provides a unique opportunity to speak the truth, however "silly," "foolish," "crazy," or "irrational" it may seem to you. Only through complete—

albeit often painful—honesty can you come to accept the validity and understand the significance of your innermost feelings.

This, of course, intimidates a great many people. Few of us are attracted to the idea of dredging up painful memories or of sharing them with a relative stranger. The good therapist, however, makes that process bearable—even, after a while, joyful. A good therapist serves in much the same way as a kindly confessor; neither urging nor chiding, he or she allows the patient to disentangle wires, to get off his or her chest things that may have been festering there for years.

Unlike the confessor, however, the therapist is a doctor, not a priest. You cannot be forgiven or absolved by your therapist. All you can receive is the ability to live your own life freely. And that, to be sure, is everything.

So the first object of the psychotherapeutic process is to *dig for clues, sift fact from fancy, and determine the sources of stress in the patient's life-style and experiences.* Toward that end, I have found it useful to seek answers to the following key questions as a guide to determining the direction of treatment.

1. What significant events have occurred in your past that may be contributing to your depression?
2. What are you doing that you don't want to do?
3. What obstacles have made it difficult for you to do what you want to do?

As the answers become clear, you will discover various patterns in your behavior that complicate your life, disrupt your relationships, intensify your guilt, and inspire negative responses to you.

The second task of therapy is to *focus on these patterns and discover ways of escaping them.* To some extent, we are all prisoners of the past, although the prisons of the severely depressed seem more tightly locked and guarded than those of "normal" people. Escape, however, is possible; it's truly amazing how many lifelong prisoners let themselves out once the therapist says simply, "Look, here's the key."

Once out, however, the real work begins, as the newly liberated person must find reasonable and productive goals to pursue—must, in short, make a life.

For some people this, and not the confessional part, is the most frightening aspect of therapy. There is no denying that, to many people, freedom is terrifying. It means added burdens, added responsibilities. And this, especially for someone who has traditionally allowed others to do his or her thinking, can be less than a pleasant prospect.

It is a prospect that so discomfits the heroine of Dr. Green's novel, for example, that she is prepared to surrender her new freedom entirely because she doesn't know how to use it. It's only after her therapist asks that she make a list of her skills and positive experiences that she is forced to see that she is capable of directing her own energies. Discovering talents she never thought she had, she is soon on the way toward defining personal goals and aspirations.

Some depressed people, on the other hand, suffer not from a deficiency of responsibility but from an abundance of it. Afraid to confront their own lives, they assume instead the burdens that rightly belong to others. Assumption of these responsibilities consumes so much energy that they have insufficient time left over for their own goals. Such "selflessness" may not only intensify a literal selflessness, or lack of ego, but lead to pent-up feelings of resentment toward the people whose burdens they have assumed.

Take Jane, for instance. The twice-divorced mother of a six-year-old boy, Jane was the consummate friend-in-need. Self-sacrificing to a fault, she helped everyone—her ex-husbands, her son, her boyfriend, her grandmother, her friends, her neighbors—everyone except herself. Nobody with a problem had to fear for assistance when Jane was around.

Inwardly, Jane seethed with resentment because she had

little energy left to pursue her own life, let alone determine what she really wanted to do with it. To disguise her distress, she turned to alcohol, and this, predictably, helped not at all. Instead, her life situation worsened. Her drinking had a bad effect on her already unhealthy relationships with those around her. There were recriminations from her family, and these made her more depressed, more dependent on the bottle.

Fortunately, one positive thing came of this situation: Jane's misery drove her to seek treatment.

The goal of therapy—and the eventual solution to Jane's problem—was for her to get rid of her unreasonable burdens and redirect her energies toward self-fulfilling activities. The third and final task of therapy is just this: to enable the patient to *refocus his or her energies on productive strategies for daily living*, based on his or her unique strengths. Achieving this goal is the central theme of all psychotherapeutic treatment.

DIGGING INTO THE PAST

The past provides clues that illuminate the present. It can shed light on the habitual patterns that keep generating unpleasant results for you. *Although the past cannot be relived or undone, it can be "defused" so that it ceases to sabotage the present—and the future.*

To do this requires taking a critical look at your early life to discover when and how negative, self-defeating patterns orginated, and to see how they continue to operate *now*. A number of themes should therefore be explored:

1. Are you still using patterns of behavior you learned in childhood to manipulate others in order to get their approval?

2. Do you have reservoirs of guilt and rage of which you are unaware?

3. Are the values you live by not really yours but those of your parents?

Once you are able to see and accept the truth about your past, you can begin to look for alternative ways to deal with the present.

That may sound easy on the face of it. All you have to do is think back and remember.

Would that it were so!

Unfortunately, it is a lot easier to recall experiences from the recent than from the distant past, and it is the distant memories that generally determine the self-defeating habits of the present. Events that occurred in the very earliest years of your life (before the age of three or four) have a decisive effect on your personality, and yet they are the most difficult to get at.

Especially in cases where the earliest experiences have been traumatic and unhappy, the first years of life may be nearly inaccessible. The mind protects itself in such cases, setting up blocks to divert and obstruct discovery. Sometimes techniques such as hypnosis must be employed to dig out the unseen demons. This method was employed with Sybil, the famous multiple personality, with the result that she is now living a productive life somewhere in the Midwest, liberated after decades of terror from the ghosts of her formative years.

Your present behavior—in particular, neurotic, inappropriate behavior—often provides clues to these past experiences. Fearfulness, uncertainty, and marked inhibition, for instance, may reflect childhood fears of parental prohibitions, now fully incorporated into your personality.

Therapy can mark the connection between past and present fears, rooting out the one and thereby defusing the other. Eventually therapy makes it possible to cleanse the personality of both damaging memories and damaging habits, so that neurotic behavior is brought to a minimum and the patient can grow in new directions.

"AM I NEUROTIC?"

In the last section, I mentioned "neurotic, inappropriate behavior." *Neurotic* is a word much bandied about these days, and it may be helpful, before going further, to define what I mean by it in this book.

Patients sometimes ask me, "I know I'm depressed, but am I neurotic?" To which I generally reply, "Probably both." For the term *neurotic* describes a thoughtlessly repetitive, sometimes obsessional mode of behavior, inherited from the past. And *depressed* is the way most neurotics feel about that behavior. The one is a reaction to the other.

All of us are neurotic to some extent. Indeed, neurosis, in certain cultural situations, may even be interpreted as a norm. Freud was not alone in perceiving a connection between the obsessional nature of primitive religious rituals and the behavior of neurotics. Both the primitive tribesman and the neurotic are caught in stereotyped, repetitive patterns. They refuse to veer away from those patterns because it seems more comfortable for them to hold onto a familiar burden than to take up the heavier, unknown cross of freedom.

This may help explain why so many couples who are unhappy together stay together in shared misery. They're accustomed to their unhappiness with each other, and they're too lethargic to change. An incident related to me recently by a patient, a fifty-year-old executive who enjoys bird watching, illustrates this point.

One winter day, he put down his newspaper and said to his wife, "Wouldn't it be nice to go to the park and see a snow owl? Want to go?"

"Not really," she replied.

So they didn't go.

But they might conceivably have gone—or at least *he* might

have gone—if he'd said, "I'm going to the park to see a snow owl. Want to come along?"

Instead, he let his wife make the decision, as he customarily does. Why? Because he doesn't want her to be angry with him—which is precisely the way he acted toward his mother when he was the coddled youngest of six children. This sheds light on why he still calls his mother three times a week. For all his years, for all his enormous success in the business world, he is still a baby in his relationship to his wife.

While he is not visibly depressed, this man clearly displays neurotic behavior—behavior that is appropriate to the past rather than the present. Therapy could help him to deal with his neurotic pattern of behavior and to be more self-assertive in his relationship with his wife. It could teach him how to pursue his interests without the fear either of devastating his wife or of being rejected by her.

When he first entered treatment, this man could barely acknowledge his anger, let alone comprehend why he was angry. In time, however, he came to see how much anger was fostered by his compliant behavior, which made it necessary for him to increase his compliance so as to hide this additional anger from her as well. Fortunately, as he changed, his wife, much to his amazement, became much more agreeable and pleasant than ever before, and their relationship began to prosper once again.

TRANSFERENCE

Transference is another term that is often misused and misunderstood. Freud felt that therapy really only began with the process of transference, and probably because he assigned it such a central role, later psychologists have tended to mystify the term, adding to his simple description an aura of mystery that suggests that what is transferred is some elusive psychic energy rather than simply the feelings the patient once had for his or her parents.

Transference is the phenomenon commonly occurring in psychotherapy in which the therapist becomes the object of unconscious feelings and attitudes previously held by the patient toward parents and others who played significant roles in the individual's life.

Actually, transference occurs all the time. Many daily situations evoke familiar yet inexplicable feelings of uncertainty, guilt, frustration, anger, or anxiety. Consider the case of a man who has trouble keeping a job because he's so sensitive to criticism he invariably loses his temper and tells off his boss. He may be acting out of a long-simmering rage toward his first "boss"—his overly strict, hypercritical father.

In treatment, such a patient, when he transferred his anger onto the therapist, would be encouraged to examine the origins of his rage and learn to stop acting out behavior appropriate to him as a child but not as an adult.

Since most of us are brought up to accept authority, transference appears frequently in our lives. When we ask others for opinions, we turn them into instant experts on whom to lean. Sometimes this leads to what might be called the "double-Marty syndrome," a situation in which two people transfer onto each other the full responsibility for a joint decision. It can lead to conversations like this:

"What do you want to do tonight?"

"I dunno, Marty, what do *you* want to do?"

"I dunno, what do *you* want to do?"

Round and round they go, neither possessing the courage to say what he'd really like to do. But suppose Marty's friend assumed the mantle of authority. Something like this might happen:

"What do you want to do tonight?"

"How about a movie, Marty?"

"Sounds okay. There's a new Robert Redford picture at the—"

"Nah, you don't want to see that. Let's catch the Western around the corner."

"Yeah, sure, why not."

Although Marty agrees, he's burning up inside because he consented to see a Western when he didn't want to. He doesn't care for Westerns. Actually, he didn't want to see a movie in the first place, but he couldn't say no for fear it might hurt his friend's feelings. If this pattern of behavior repeats itself often enough, it can lead to depression.

In my own practice, in general I believe in being supportive of patients while encouraging them to decide what is really important to them—regardless of what others think—and to focus all their energies on achieving it.

This is a matter of urgency for depressed and suicidal patients because they tend to be so bereft of a sense of self-worth that they are often totally dependent on what someone else thinks of them.

RECOVERING THE EGO

The Polish novelist Witold Gombrowicz's masterpiece, *Fer-dydurke*, describes the reversion of a young adult man to the attitudes and behavior of an adolescent, merely in response to the opinions of acquaintances who tell him he is acting like a child. Internalizing their criticism, he makes it prophetic; by the end of the novel he has changed completely into what they tell him he is.

This is an example of severely neurotic behavior, a type of reaction all too common among the depressed. Almost without exception, the very depressed allow others to make decisions for them. They surrender control to friends and relatives, then to fantasies and memory, and finally to the voracious, unforgiving past itself.

The typical suicidal patient who enters my office for the first time would fit a profile like this:

The patient is not in control of his life at the moment. He is, in fact, not living in the present—which, in a sense, is not being alive at all. Nor is he living in the past (although he is controlled by it) or in the future; he is nowhere. He is afraid of asserting himself. To win approval (which he will mistrust when it is given), he takes on other people's burdens, then feels imposed upon by them. He hasn't the confidence to say or do what he wants, for fear someone might be offended; and that would make him anxious. The only act of ego left for him is to kill himself. Even then, what he really wants to kill is merely a *part* of himself—the part he loathes and feels guilty about because it is a reflection of the negative things he feels others think of him.

Anne Sexton, the Pulitzer Prize poet who suffered from severe depression, which led to her suicide in 1974, once said, "I need my husband and children . . . to tell me who I am."

With Anne Sexton, as with all people, the first people to tell you "who you are" are your parents.

Suppose a child takes a cookie from the cookie jar. Her mother catches her in the act and says sternly as she slaps her daughter's hand, "Bad Suzy! You mustn't take a cookie without permission. Bad Suzy!" The next time the child gets caught raiding the cookie jar, she herself says, "Bad Suzy!" before her mother can utter a word—an act of contrition for which she is duly praised.

In other words, not only does Suzy develop an image of herself as "bad," but she also learns that to punish or criticize herself is less painful than having someone else do it. Moreover, she is *rewarded* for being self-punishing. Thus, her *superego* (that inner watchdog) keeps riding herd on her *ego* (sense of self), forever cautioning, "Uh-uh ... better not ... you'll be punished ... bad Suzy!"

Such negative early exposure to stern, if not punitive and unforgiving, parental values and attitudes can badly cripple one's sense of self-esteem.

While a strong, healthy sense of self is a reliable instrument for processing incoming data from the environment and making suitable decisions, a weak, fragile self misreads such data. Because it distorts the truth, it cannot cope adequately with everyday problems, let alone real stress.

Psychotherapy seeks to strengthen the ego and reduce the distortion of reality on the assumption that reality creates fewer problems than does illusion. Innovation by a strong self, psychotherapy believes, is healthier than being governed by habit.

TAKING CARE OF YOU

Learning to take care of yourself constitutes a major focus of treatment. If you feel obligated to take on responsibility for others, you must be helped to see that this can be done satisfactorily only *after* you take care of your own life first.

This is not a justification for brutalizing or ignoring others. It means that you must not undertake responsibilities for others that are greater than those you undertake for yourself.

Which is what Clara had to learn.

Clara was fifty-three when she entered treatment. Although she had never actually tried to end her life, she periodically felt very suicidal. Her age, divorced status, and propensity to excessive drinking pointed to a real risk of suicide.

Five years previously, her husband had divorced her, leaving her with three children, ages fourteen to twenty. Her children, troubled by the divorce, made heavy demands on her. Because of her propensity to "sacrifice" for others, she

tried to meet their expectations, but failed, and was in continual conflict with her children. "They show me no respect," she
complained.

In part, Clara's children may have been mirroring her poor
opinion of herself. A college graduate, she was nevertheless
working at an undemanding clerical job. In addition, the more
rejected she felt, the more she drank.

Strengthening Clara's ego and reducing her need for masochistic ways of relating to people became a primary task of
treatment. It was important to get her to see how she kept
setting up situations that inevitably brought rejection.

On one occasion, her children invited her out to dinner for
her birthday and asked her to choose a restaurant. Her
response was that she didn't feel like being taken out to dinner,
and besides, weren't they cruel, ungrateful children, anyway?

They had extended an olive branch to her, and she had
rejected it outright. Not surprisingly, this elicited a hostile
response from her children.

Their invitation, on the other hand, was probably a complex
mixture: part peace offering, part affectionate gesture, and
part strategy for winning her over so they could continue to
make heavy demands on her.

If, as Clara claimed, she really wanted to reduce both their
dependency upon her and her willingness to accept it, she
should have said, "Yes, I'd like that," or "Sorry, I've other
plans," or simply, "Thank you, I'd rather not." Instead, she
ensured that the mutual hostility and dependence that characterized their unhappy relationship would continue. Her usual
martyr's response provoked them once again to reject her.

In treatment, Clara began to see how she was using hostility
much as a child does: as a way of manipulating others to gain
approval. If she made her children feel guilty, then they would
be extra nice to her, treating her, in essence, like a hurt child.

One day Clara said to me, "So much of their attitude is that
they're the parents and I'm the child." As Clara was beginning

to realize, she courted that response. Gradually she improved, and today she is doing quite well, acting more freely and assertively because she is responding to her children in an adult way.

THE MARTYR'S HOOK

The mixture of hostility and dependence that characterized Clara's stormy relationship with her children is not uncommon. A typical exchange:

"I'd behave differently if you were *nicer* to me," says A. to B. Then, tugging on B.'s guilt-strings, A. recites a litany of accumulated gripes. If B.'s decisions on how to behave are then governed by the way A. responds, B. is not acting freely, but is dependent on A. Furthermore, by trying to manipulate B., A. invites *mutual* dependence.

Parents often unwittingly manipulate their children in this fashion under the guise of disciplining them or telling them what to do "for their own good."

The dynamics of such interactions are intricate and subtle. It is not easy to see what is really going on. Try to appraise your own behavior realistically, particularly in those relationships that consistently elicit negative responses from others. If you take responsibility for the negative behavior of others, making sacrifices in an effort to appease them, you are acting as a martyr. This inevitably proves harmful, especially if you then attribute your distress not to your own actions but to the demands of others.

Martyrs are no fun to be with, and their sacrifices are hardly ever appreciated. People usually sense the hostility, resentment, and manipulation behind a compulsion to meet others' expectations.

Consider this typical scene:

"How about that Italian restaurant?" suggests Joe.

"Wouldn't you rather have French food?" Jane counters.

"I hate French food," says Joe.

"And I'm on a diet," says Jane.

"Tell you what," says Joe, "I'll go along with you if you go along with me. Let's have Italian food tonight, and French food tomorrow night."

A good compromise, you think? Wrong. It's a terrible compromise because both Joe and Jane will resent part of it. Even if only one of them resented it, the compromise would be a bad one, for it would have aroused feelings of anger and guilt—the old superego again, whispering, "Shame, shame . . . getting angry over a *restaurant!*"

A *genuine* compromise would be for Joe and Jane to pick a third restaurant—one they *both* liked.

The lesson here is that you should always make an effort to define for yourself what *you* like and want. Unfortunately, few people question the assumption that it is best to "go along in the spirit of cooperation" with things they actually find repugnant. More harm is done in the name of friendship, loyalty, patriotism, and "not making waves" than most of us realize.

THE GENTLE ART OF AVOIDANCE

The ostensibly violent martial art of jujitsu is based, paradoxically, on the principle of yielding to rather than combating aggression. The word *jujitsu* means, in fact, "the gentle art," and its central notion is that the person who is able to give way gracefully will be more successful than the person who is concerned only with winning, with knocking his or her head against a wall.

This "gentle art" has an analogy in daily life. Many depressed patients have to learn that health often lies not along a path of constant effort, but along the line of least resistance.

Getting patients to accept the fact that they don't *have* to fight themselves and "go along"—that, indeed, they can, and often should, *withdraw* from obligations imposed upon them by others—is one of the most challenging tasks facing the therapist.

When depressed people feel exhausted, they need a chance to withdraw. They need to understand that it is unnecessary for them to take on additional challenges.

When people get *physically* ill, they are usually encouraged to take to their beds to allow their systems to recover. But such good advice is rarely given to people suffering from emotional illness. If you break your leg and hobble around in a cast, people will say, "Take it easy . . . go slow." But if you're hobbled by depression, they'll say, "Hey! Snap out of it!" This kind of advice seldom does anything but aggravate the depression.

There's nothing wrong with taking a "sick day" off when you're terribly depressed. Such a modest form of hibernation runs counter to the Puritan ethic, however. The conventional wisdom is: Work harder and you'll work it out. Instead, my advice is:

Build a little vacation into your life.

Crawl into bed and pull the covers over you.

Go ahead, it's all right.

In my view, the Taoist notion of bypassing pressure—the philosophy behind jujitsu—makes a great deal of sense.

FLIGHT VERSUS FIGHT

You are probably familiar with the "fight-or-flight" response; at some time or other, you have undoubtedly experienced it. It is the way the body gears itself to face a threat. The heart pounds, there's an empty feeling in the stomach, and there's a lightheaded sensation as the system pumps adrenaline into the bloodstream.

Whether you respond to a threat, real or imagined, by

fighting (lashing out) or fleeing (running or even fainting) depends on your attitude, training, and experience.

The first time someone insults you, for instance, your impulse might be to insult the other person back.

This generally escalates conflict. Once you are aware of your response pattern, however, you can, if that person insults you again, *withhold your reaction*. By containing yourself, you allow your physiological juices to cool down. Then you can decide if you care to dignify the insult with a counterinsult or by staying calm avoid a meaningless or unwanted conflict.

Unfortunately, fleeing or avoiding conflict is often regarded as cowardice in our culture. But if you're depressed, it may be the better part of wisdom.

The high suicide rate among men in Finland, for example, stems in part from a tradition in which men learn never to admit their failings openly. If a Finn past fifty loses his job and feels dejected, he's expected to act as if nothing has happened, to continue to act strong—in other words, to "fight." When he feels so beaten down by the world that he can't take it, he can do the "manly" thing—kill himself. By such a standard, suicide is understandable, an accepted tradition.

Suicide is not "flight," but a twisted form of "fight"—a futile and indirect lashing out at the world and at those who have hurt you. What makes a person suicidal is trying to function as if he or she feels normal and strong when in fact the individual feels terrible.

GETTING THE WORLD OFF YOUR BACK

It often happens that at the very time of a suicide attempt the person is very involved in providing help for others but is inwardly raging.

An excellent example is the case of Arnold, a fairly successful actor whose wife was having an affair with another man.

Not only had Arnold moved out of the house at her insistence, but he continued to support her extravagant life-style. When she demanded money for the upkeep of the house, he provided it. To please her, he even allowed her to drive their Rolls-Royce while he drove their old car.

"Why do you allow yourself to be dumped on?" I asked him. I pointed out that by acquiescing to her demands, he was letting his wife define his responsibilities.

One day shortly thereafter, Arnold spotted their Rolls parked in front of her lover's house. He then did something uncharacteristic for him. He drove off with the car. This improved his spirits somewhat, but he was still essentially unhappy.

"If you're miserable where you are, go where you're *less* miserable," I advised him.

"But she doesn't want me at home," was Arnold's reply.

"That's *her* problem," I told him.

So Arnold moved back home—which thoroughly unsettled his wife. But as a result of his uncharacteristically asserting himself, Arnold and his wife began to work things out.

It's fine to be your brother's keeper, but *be your own keeper first*. This is not being selfish—nor is selfishness the antidote to selflessness. What being your own keeper amounts to is self-preservation.

EXTERNALIZING THE PROBLEM

Before you and your therapist can examine what's truly bothering you, it's necessary to *externalize* your problem—that is, take it outside of yourself so you can look at it objectively. Sometimes the therapist will have to pull it out of you bit by bit.

I was once awakened at four A.M. by a patient telephoning to complain that her husband's ex-wife had phoned *her* at eight thirty the previous morning to say his daughter (of the first marriage) might be suspended from school for smoking marijuana.

"Can you imagine the effect that news will have on my husband? And imagine the nerve of her calling me at eight thirty in the morning to tell me *that!*" she grumbled.

My patient continued to rehash this and other incidents involving the ex-wife. However, she neglected to get to the point, the issue that was really bothering her. It took me nearly an hour to find out what it was. After six years of marriage, the patient felt that she was not fully accepted by her husband. She felt her marriage was threatened by his ex-wife, who was still trying to maintain ties with her former husband.

Once she could admit this, she was able to examine her relationship with her husband—and his ex-wife—more realistically. She was also able to begin to come to terms with the various ways her own behavior was driving a wedge between herself and her husband.

I don't want to suggest that one such insight is all it takes to cure a depression. The therapeutic process may have its share of dramatic episodes, but it is more painstaking than fictional psychotherapy would lead you to believe. Becoming aware of how much abuse you absorb from others, and of the need to avoid such pressures, is merely the first step. Putting your insights to work for you takes time.

COPING WITH STRESS

One of the secrets of avoiding stress is to try not to react immediately. Instead, focus on what others are really saying. Consider, for example, the telephone—a major instrument of stress.

We often get and transmit aggravation by phone. Some

people actually hate to answer the phone. Others, by rattling on and on without getting to the point, can inflict enormous stress on a listener. By not reacting to stress, I don't mean to suggest that you not answer your telephone or that you hang up on a stressful caller. Rather, you might try an approach that has proved successful for many:

1. Keep a pad and pencil near the phone to take notes of the conversation.

2. Don't hesitate to clarify what you don't understand by asking others to repeat what they have said.

3. If you feel an argument coming on, *don't react. Listen.* (If you're writing down what is being said, you'll find that you *are* listening. You have to.)

Using this method of defusing potential antagonism, you should find that your whole rhythm of responses will change. The other person will receive a different set of cues from you, and this will demand a different response from your caller.

This technique can be especially effective with those who try to get you to solve their problems by assuming responsibility for them. When you withhold your reaction and *listen*, you'll find they often begin to suggest solutions themselves without needing to have you tell them what to do.

Moreover, you'll begin to *hear* what the other person is really trying to say. Consequently, your responses can be more to the point. Instead of mumbling your appreciation of how nice it was for your friend to call, you can admit what you hear "between the lines" and say, "You're pretty annoyed that I missed your birthday party, aren't you?"

In face-to-face encounters, where a pad and pencil would be awkward, *body language* (gestures, facial expressions, posture) provides clues to what is actually being communicated. Since much has been written elsewhere on the subject, I wish merely to point out the value of being alert to body-language signals transmitted *to* you and *by* you. If, for example, your sagging posture conveys your negative expectations—even subliminally—you're apt to get a negative response.

In coping with stress, electronic technology has opened up an exciting area of treatment for many emotional and physical ailments: biofeedback training (BFT).

BFT involves two principal steps: *relaxation training* and *biofeedback*, or the monitoring of certain biological responses—for example, brainwave rhythms—while a visible or audible signal—for example, a beeping sound—tells you how relaxed you really are. Using the method to combat stress, some patients have learned to lower their blood pressure, slow a racing heartbeat, relieve migraine headaches, stop asthma attacks, and cure stuttering. In my own practice, I have found BFT invaluable in helping patients to overcome phobias—such as a fear of dogs or of taking medicine—and to control or stop panic symptoms.

Once you discover how quickly you can gain control over your inner responses by externalizing them (watching the feedback signal), you will be more capable of controlling your automatic responses to threatening situations, thereby increasing your capacity to cope with stress and to control your life.

MAXIMIZING YOUR CHOICES

As you reach an understanding of your depression and how you may be contributing to it, and as you learn to control your reactions to stress, you are ready for the next step: choosing your goals.

The choice is yours. The determination to choose your goals (and the courage to make mistakes while you work toward them) now becomes the focus of treatment.

Consider Gabrielle. Everybody envied Gabrielle and her husband, Paul. They were the perfect couple, very attached, united in love and work. But behind the idyllic façade, the marriage was disintegrating. So was Gabrielle.

She had emigrated to the United States from France in the mid-1950s, when she was twenty-three. A year later, she married Paul, an accountant fifteen years her senior.

At the time, she was earning a modest income as a dressmaker. But soon Gabrielle began moving up—first to a job as a dressmaker/saleswoman in a smart boutique, then eventually to a small boutique of her own. The boutique thrived. One shop grew to two. Before long, Paul was working for *her*.

To their friends, they continued to appear a doting couple, but Paul felt emasculated. He yearned for more control over the business.

And he began "playing around."

In 1970, Gabrielle flew to France to visit her sister, who was dying of cancer. When she returned, she discovered evidence in the apartment that convinced her that Paul had been philandering. They fought, and he admitted that he had been having an affair. They discussed the possibility of a divorce.

Gabrielle's problems seemed to accelerate from that point on. She was hospitalized with an ulcer, only to learn, upon recovering, that Paul had stolen part of the business. It was the final straw. She obtained a divorce.

Now Gabrielle was plagued by feelings of frustration and abandonment. Although rejected by Paul, she also felt guilty about having rejected him. At the same time, still upset over her sister's illness, Gabrielle became obsessed by a fear that she, too, was dying of cancer. One evening, after closing her shop—from which she no longer derived much sense of fulfillment—she went home and deliberately took an overdose of barbiturates and alcohol. Fortunately, the dose was not fatal, and after this episode she sought therapy.

When Gabrielle became my patient, one of my first tasks was to help her reconcile herself to the divorce, as well as recognize that the disintegration of the marriage had been occurring bit by bit over the years. As a matter of fact, Gabrielle had been drinking on and off for some time.

Paul even seemed to have been grateful for her drinking bouts, for then he could surmount his sense of inadequacy by taking care of her and covering for her with friends and business associates.

At first, she appreciated these attentions; then she began to resent them. Finally, in confusion over her own feelings, she turned obnoxious and abused him.

Gabrielle took a significant step toward externalizing her problem one day when she decided to visit her ex-husband to test her reaction to him. The visit gave her a perspective she had never had before, for during it she realized how dependent and immature Paul had always been.

Once her guilt over the divorce lessened (and with it the guilt that had operated through the years each time he made dependent demands on her by appealing to her sense of responsibility), she could face what to her was an astonishing truth:

She never could tolerate his dependency. She had *wanted* to be divorced.

Her newfound sense of independence was mystifying to her. She wondered how she ever could have feared that she couldn't get along without Paul. Clearly, she *preferred* to be without him. The possibility that he had never loved her, and that she might mistakenly have loved him, was no longer too painful to admit.

Gabrielle faced another difficult truth. Her uncertainty over her future because of the divorce, as well as her sister's (and her own) health, was just a trigger for the suicide attempt.

The cause could be traced to her childhood. The youngest in a large family, Gabrielle had been a pampered, spoiled child who came to expect that she ought to be catered to, and she manipulated others to get her way. In adulthood, her frustration and impotent rage at being rejected led to her wish to die.

With treatment, however, she was able to exorcise the ghosts of the past and take a realistic look at her present situation.

My role during this stage of treatment was to support Gabrielle in her new, though occasionally shaky, resolve to set new goals.

I did this by encouraging her to develop new life strategies that would give her greater mastery over herself and her environment. And finally, I had to help her to mobilize her energies toward achieving her goals.

To a great extent, she already has. Today, Gabrielle enjoys her work more than ever. Her business is prospering, and she appears to relish her new, more independent life-style.

MOBILIZING YOUR ENERGIES

At some point in your treatment, the central arena for growth will be, as with Gabrielle, the achievement of your *personal goals.* You should be aware that efforts to modify your behavior and objectives may create anxiety and resistance in others—especially those who are comfortable with the "old" you. Sometimes, the more you get the world off your back, the more it tries to climb back on.

Treatment at this stage explores obstacles to the attainment of goals and seeks to facilitate change by harnessing your special strengths.

Once you start moving toward a goal, you may be stymied by the passive resistance of those whom you used to try to influence or manipulate. You may be thrown off balance by new, unfamiliar cues in your changing situation. You may find yourself stopped in your tracks by flattery, cajolery, even threats or commands from others. Envy and competitiveness may distract you from your objectives. Angered and over-whelmed by this interference, you may feel inclined to rebel and act against your own best interests, often in countless small ways: failing to prepare for your changing options, preoccupying yourself with trivial matters, avoiding new activities, doing anything that perpetuates your state of inertia.

For these reasons, it is wise not to try to "go for broke," gambling all your energies on a grand-slam bid for change. That would be an invitation to be beaten down—which is the way a depressed patient feels to begin with.

So ease slowly into independence by asking yourself:

1. What *can* I do?
2. What are the things I *can* control?

When you have answered these questions, you will be better able to act in your own behalf.

DO IT YOURSELF

I said at the outset of this chapter that psychotherapy was not designed to trip you up or fix blame for your past failings, but to help you discover your strengths, to discover yourself.

Finally, of course, only one person can tell you who you are, and that person is you.

The ultimate goal of therapy, therefore, is to enable you to concentrate on what you *want* to do, rather than on what others—including the therapist—think you *ought* to do. Effective therapy brings you to the point where it makes itself unnecessary. Its ideal is to create free human beings, people who are animated rather than intimidated by the injunction "Do it yourself."

At the same time, a growth in independent competence can help you to be more giving and understanding of others. Freed from the constraint to gain their approval, you will be able to meet them in a confident, rather than nervous, selflessness.

The more you show interest in others and the more you recognize their needs and offer some comfort—without compromising yourself—the more satisfied you will feel. Seeking out the positive qualities in others and praising them when they merit praise will improve and solidify relationships.

Listen to what others have to say. This will help you discover their positive features. It will also alert you to ways in which you can be of help to them, as well as ways in which your relationships can become mutually satisfying. Your acting positively toward others will encourage them to react positively toward you.

You must always, of course, be alert to what limits you should impose on your behavior. Discover the extent to which you can overcome the need to act in terms of other people's needs, and thus be in a position to act freely. To act freely—to become what you are capable of becoming—is the best definition I know for the courage to live.

6

A Guide for Family and Friends

What do we live for, if it is not to make life less difficult
for each other?

—GEORGE ELIOT

In the last chapter, I asked you to put yourself in the role of a
patient. Now I ask you to switch roles and become what
therapists call a *significant other*.

A significant other is anyone who is an important person in
the patient's life, be it spouse, parent, child, sibling, lover, close
friend, or boss. By extension, a firm, a social institution, a class
of people, or an unreachable goal can also function as a
significant other.

As a significant other—especially a close friend or family
member—you should learn as much as possible about the
nature of the treatment the patient is receiving, not only for
the patient's sake but for your own as well. Psychotherapy is
not a track on which one runs a steady course from sickness to
health. Instead, patients usually zigzag, at times stumbling and
falling. Setbacks are to be expected. These setbacks can create
doubt and tension concerning the value of therapy, intensifying the general fear and indecision already felt by the patient.
Such doubts, reinforced by the reappearance of depressive

symptoms, sometimes lead relatives and friends to conclude that the treatment isn't working. This reaction encourages any inclination of the patient to mistrust the therapeutic process, and ultimately undermines the therapy.

While such a reaction is understandable, given the time and expense involved in much private therapy it is a shame that impatience and frustration often lead well-meaning relatives—and even patients themselves—to terminate treatment at the first signs of slowness or regression. Hard as it seems, you as a significant other must practice patience if therapy is to be truly effective. We still know very little about how long individual treatments will take, and predictions of the time involved are unreliable. Some persons are cured of their depressions within a matter of months, while therapy in other cases can take years.

All I can say, as a psychotherapist who has treated literally thousands of suicidal patients, is that faith in the therapeutic process can go a long way toward shortening the duration of treatment. Grumbling on the part of significant others can only retard the process, while intelligent, supportive attitudes can bolster the patient's confidence and sustain him or her through the worst periods of despair.

In many instances, I find it valuable, if not urgent, to involve members of the immediate family in the treatment process. This involvement may take the form of private talks and/or family therapy sessions. Such involvement helps the family to understand the importance and desirability of treatment and to overcome any notions that mental illness carries a ocial stigma.

When possible, I include significant family members even in the initial evaluation of the patient in order to determine their attitudes toward the patient, the illness, and the treatment. I also want to ensure that manipulative and judgmental attitudes will be minimized. If you happen to be a member of a depressed patient's immediate family, you should understand that a supportive, noncritical attitude on your part can have an enormously favorable effect on the outcome of therapy.

DON'T FEEL GUILTY

When chatting with family members during the initial interview, or after a patient has had a relapse, I often hear cries of self-reproach such as these: "Oh, if I hadn't said those terrible things . . . " "If only I hadn't hung up the phone . . . " "If I hadn't broken our date . . ." Invariably, the speakers want to know if they're responsible in some way for the patient's condition.

This is understandable. Depression seems, much more than mere physical illness, a socially induced disease—something conditioned and perhaps even caused by the depressed person's contact with others. It is not outlandish to assume, therefore, if you have had significant contact with a depressed person, that at least part of his or her problem may be your fault. Frequently, significant others torture themselves on this account with a barrage of self-recriminating questions ("What did I do to bring this about?"), seeking either to vindicate themselves or to confirm their culpability for the depression.

With rare exceptions, however, the evidence suggests that significant others do *not* cause psychiatric illness. They can, either consciously or unwittingly, worsen an illness by intensifying the victim's guilt and anxiety. They can aggravate a bad condition by adopting reproachful or reprimanding attitudes. I certainly do not mean to suggest that saying "terrible things" or hanging up on a severely depressed person will *help* matters at all. If your overall *pattern* of behavior toward the patient is characterized chiefly by such negative reactions, you may indeed be a contributing factor to the depression.

But not the cause.

As already noted, depression develops from a complex

combination of physical, biochemical, psychological, and social factors that combine to make certain individuals susceptible to depression under certain kinds of stress. No one person can be blamed for that susceptibility.

Feeling guilty or blaming yourself is therefore a waste of emotional energy. Being preoccupied with guilt and self-blame is unproductive, if not counterproductive. Instead of blaming yourself, you should learn how to *stop* contributing to the patient's problem.

My experience has shown that relatives and friends of depressed persons generally make one of two major errors. The first is the one I have just discussed: that of blaming themselves for the problem. The other is to go to an opposite extreme and deny that the problem exists. Rather than acknowledge the problem, they put on heavy blinders.

WEARING BLINDERS

Depression does not always appear abruptly in all its intensity. Often the illness builds gradually, so that what at first seems merely a case of the "blahs" turns in time, and almost imperceptibly, into a full-fledged depressive neurosis. So gradual can the deepening of despair seem to outside observers that they often fail to identify it until it is far advanced.

In addition, the social stigma that unfortunately still attaches to mental illness in this "enlightened" age often makes it easy for even close observers to close their eyes to a growing depression and convince themselves that what is happening is "not that serious" or that it will "pass away in time."

Moreover, patients are frequently quite willing to cooperate in this conspiracy of silence because they are both afraid and ashamed of what is happening to them. This in turn makes it easier for significant others to go on wearing blinders. In some cases this ostensibly benign neglect of the issue takes the form of outright denial: "There's nothing wrong with him that a few days' fishing won't cure." Or, "She's just tired. She'll snap out of it."

Minimizing the need for help and actually denying the existence of the problem share a common root: they allow the parties who ought to be concerned to get off the hook by denying their responsibility for the situation. If there is no illness, they need feel no guilt.

It's difficult, of course, to identify exactly when the blahs have become a case of chronic blues—exactly when a person needs help. But as a general rule of thumb I would say that any depression that lasts more than a month or so warrants professional investigation.

THE "SICK ROLE"

One of the most important things you can do as a concerned relative or friend is to help someone suffering from depressive illness to *accept* the "sick role," or "patient role," if he or she has difficulty in doing so.

An acknowledgment of illness and a recognition of the need for professional help are critical components of a general willingness to accept that role—that is, to enter treatment, remain in it, and become fully engaged in psychotherapy.

Regrettably, some patients enter and remain in treatment *while denying their need for it*. They never fully accept the patient role. Obviously, this works against effective treatment, for the way patients view their illnesses and the need for treatment has a direct bearing on the *outcome* of treatment.

THE DROPOUTS

The proportion of patients who fail to remain in treatment long enough to achieve significant results is alarmingly high. The support of family and friends might help to decrease this dropout rate and thus increase the chances of improvement.

In a long-term follow-up study of some six hundred depressed and suicidal patients, I found that they fell into seven cluster types. Two types are in particular need of understanding and support from family and friends. These two types—a constant source of frustration for therapists—include those patients most likely to drop out of treatment. The two types share an interesting quality: a discrepancy between their views of their illness and how they interact with significant others, and the views of the significant others.

In one syndrome, the patient maximizes the gravity of his problem while the significant others minimize it. You can well understand how such a reaction could demoralize and deflate a depressed person. An equivalent reaction to a purely physical illness would be unthinkable. Imagine, for example, saying to a person suffering from migraine headaches, "Oh, they can't be all that bad." Predictably, such comments are generally interpreted by depressed patients as evidence of indifference or rejection.

The other syndrome is the reverse. The patient minimizes the gravity of his problem while the significant others maximize it. In one of my cases, a young man in his late teens was under considerable pressure from his parents, who thought him sicker than he was. They may have been overreacting to their son's blithe insistence that "There's nothing wrong with me." In any event, the parents became overcontrolling, which angered the young man, who interpreted their behavior as punishment. Recognizing that the patient was a potential dropout, I conducted a series of family therapy sessions to bridge the gulf of misunderstanding between parents and son.

Patients displaying both these syndromes are high suicide risks. Feeling themselves misunderstood, they invariably choose irreversible means and private, often remote, places for their suicide attempts. Such patients, moreover, may *already* have isolated themselves socially by the time of their suicide attempt. Therefore, significant others are less likely to be aware of their depressive symptoms.

The two types I've described are hard to treat. It is typical of them to see a therapist two or three times and then not return. They're usually uncooperative as well, and as manipulative of the therapist as they are of the people close to them.

I recall a librarian in her late twenties—I'll call her Joan—who was extremely phobic and easily panicked. She lived with her parents, and since she was afraid to go to work by herself, her mother drove her.

Through the years, she had seen a number of therapists, never for any length of time. No doubt she played the same manipulative, controlling game with them as she tried with me. For instance, she would agree to take her medicine, then call to say she didn't want to take it. She would make appointments, then call to postpone them.

The degree to which Joan's parents contributed to and sustained her illness became vividly clear at a family session soon after she was referred to me. I had suggested that Joan's mother not drive her to work anymore.

"Then she won't go at all," her mother objected.

"Fine," I told her. "If she doesn't feel like going, let her take some time off. When she's ready to go back, let her do so on her own. It's her responsibility."

I also pointed out that it would be good for the mother to stop serving as her daughter's chauffeur and "do her own thing" for a change.

At this point, Joan's father objected. He thought it preferable that Joan keep working and that the family not give in to her "moods." As he continued in this vein, Joan became anxious and began to breathe rapidly.

Apparently insensitive to her distress, oblivious even to her rapid, increasingly audible gasps for breath, her father kept right on talking. His denial of her illness was so complete that he dared not recognize any evidence to the contrary.

This was obviously an impossible situation. Treatment of such a disturbed individual would have been hard enough even with the full cooperation of all parties concerned. The father's intransigence, however, complicated matters beyond reparation. For several more weeks I attempted to enlist his support for Joan's behalf, but he remained adamant, convinced that she was just "faking it." Eventually, with great regret, I had to recognize that the patient was not ready to enter treatment, and I resigned.

Without the cooperation of significant others, sometimes even the therapist must become a dropout.

A FAMILY PROBLEM

In 1970 British therapist R. D. Laing came up with an innovative theory to explain the appearance in certain families of not one but two or more severely disturbed individuals. In his book *Sanity, Madness, and the Family* he suggests that mental disorder, while it may sometimes have a genetic or biochemical base, is often aggravated, even induced, by inherently pathological family structures.

He cites many cases of ostensibly "inherited" psychosis, only to debunk the inheritance thesis by demonstrating how circumstances within the families involved—including double or conflicting messages, obstructive and brutal behavior, and indifferent or hostile emotional responses—were sufficient in themselves to induce psychotic behavior in family members who in other circumstances might have grown up entirely healthy.

Joan's father may be cited as a case in point. There is no way of telling how severely his refusal to admit that his daughter was ill may have added to her stress, but that the refusal *was* stressful for her was obvious from the fact that her bout of acute hyperventilation followed immediately upon his dismissal of her sickness.

An understanding of the home situation is therefore very valuable to the therapist in determining the causes, both past and immediate, of the patient's malaise. Indeed, since significant others can play such an important role in the treatment process, especially in the early phases, it is sometimes useful for close relatives to *enter psychotherapy themselves* at the same time as the patient in order to understand their own anxieties and how they contribute to the patient's problems. Certainly, this would have benefited Joan's parents and, ultimately, Joan herself.

Ruth was a somewhat different case. Although her parents did not enter therapy on their own, I did meet with them for at least ten minutes every time I saw their daughter.

Ruth was eighteen when they first brought her to my office. I was immediately struck by her wooden manner and the mechanical way she kept apologizing when she had nothing to apologize about. Ruth was intensely phobic, ritualistic, and supersensitive. Her fearful, distorted perceptions of her environment caused her to overreact to events around her, and this in turn insulated her from reality.

During talks with her parents, I learned that Ruth's extremely overprotective mother was also plagued by depressions, as was *her* mother. Ruth's father, a complex neurotic in his own right, admitted that his marriage was a very unhappy one. Clearly, for Ruth's sake at least, her home environment had to improve.

Intensive therapy over time, with the parents involved in the preliminary ten-minute sessions, did improve the situation, and Ruth herself became less depressed and more assertive. As she changed, I helped her parents go through the changes with her. So successful was this process, in fact, that there is an ironic footnote to Ruth's story. Some months after she had improved enough to forgo regular weekly treatment sessions, her parents brought her in again complaining that Ruth was carrying her newfound assertiveness too far and had become unbearably aggressive. With some wryness I had to make clear to Ruth that being independent did not mean that she had a right to be nasty.

HOW SHOULD YOU ACT?

Keep in mind that many depressed people are irritable to begin with, and that even the meek can become overbearing if their developing ego muscle gets flexed all the time. However, blaming them for the strained relationships that result, or uttering an impatient "Oh, snap out of it!" can be devastating. These reactions will doubtless be heard by the depressed person as expressions of anger, which indeed they may be.

Each of us has a fundamental need for emotional support from family and friends. In a depressed or suicidal person that need is exaggerated. Rejection, hostility, or merely a lack of concern can be especially demoralizing to someone whom depression has made vulnerable.

Just as demoralizing to the emotionally disturbed can be the lack of adequate understanding of the individual's behavior that leads relatives and friends to apply *too much* pressure. The depressed or suicidal person may interpret this, as well, as criticism or rejection.

Striking the right balance between a lack of concern and too much concern can be tricky. Think of how you feel when you have a splitting headache. It's comforting to know someone is around in case you need anything, but you don't want to get into a major discussion about it.

How *should* you behave, then, with a person who is severely depressed?

Ironically, the approach taken by many people—the approach that any of us would take as a matter of course with a normally healthy person with the blues—is exactly the wrong one to adopt with a seriously depressed person.

When most of us are feeling "down," we often try to divert our attention from our blues by involving ourselves in some outside activity, such as a movie or a sports event. And for most of us, this works quite well. But it does not work, and it therefore makes no sense, for someone in the throes of severe depression.

Chronic or suicidal depression cannot be whisked away by an entertaining diversion, and the suggestion that it can is likely to strike the depressed person not as imaginative and caring but as either insensitive or beside the point.

Actually, the worst thing to say to the victim of depression would be something like "Come on! Stop mooning around. Let's see a movie. It'll make you feel better." It would be much wiser for you—without pushing—to get the individual to tell you how he or she feels, to listen patiently, and then to say, "Too bad you're feeling this way. If there's anything I can do, I'll be here."

Sometimes the way to be most helpful is to let the person just be.

However, you might mention that depression is self–limiting and that he or she *will* come out of it. Or if the person has been depressed for a month or more without contemplating treatment, it would be appropriate, for instance, to say, "Depression *can* be treated—there are medicines that can relieve the way you feel. You *will* get better with the proper help."

This can be very reassuring. You might also mention that the depressed person is in good company. Abraham Lincoln, Nathaniel Hawthorne, Winston Churchill, astronaut Buzz Aldrin, and even Sigmund Freud suffered from severe depression.

And overcame it.

Should there be a suicide attempt, the same precepts apply. Don't exert pressure, but don't turn your back on the problem, either. The reaction of family and friends to suicide threats, more often than not, is to withdraw out of helplessness, fear, or disgust, or else to try to talk the individual out of it. This only confirms the suicidal person's conviction that "Nobody understands me."

Look at it this way. Suppose you fell and fractured your leg.

How would you feel if friends walked by and pretended not to notice? Or if they snapped, "Quit lying there! Get up and walk!" But you'd be relieved to hear: "Do you think you can get up? If you can't, take it easy. Help is on its way."

It's crucial to recognize the importance of allowing the patient's own state of mind to determine the degree of his or her activity or inactivity. People who are mildly depressed or recovering from a serious depression will probably benefit from keeping busy. Challenging work, exercise, a new hobby, good company, a change of scene—these can act as a tonic. But only the patient truly knows how much activity and/or pressure he or she can tolerate, and the attempts of solicitous friends to get the patient "moving again" before the time is ripe can be damaging rather than productive.

I once treated an elderly gentleman who had been an active businessman until he suffered a minor stroke. His wife and children promptly created an institutional setting at home and began acting like baby-sitters. This increased his feeling of impotence, associated with his inability to function as vigorously as before. While preventing him from going to work, they nevertheless pushed him to get up and go out. "Keep yourself busy," they would say.

They would have been wiser to let him take things easy until he was ready for more activity. Often, in such a setting, a patient will make a suicide attempt. (This patient had begun to *talk* of suicide.) When his family was persuaded to adopt an easygoing posture toward him, his depression gradually lifted and he returned to work.

THE SELF-FULFILLING PROPHECY

Without realizing it, significant others can communicate negative expectations that take on a life of their own. A young woman I treated had trouble having a successful relationship with a man. Whenever she began a new relationship, she discussed it with her mother, and her mother, in various ways, conveyed doubt as to its outcome. When the relationship didn't work out, the mother would always say, "I told you so."

To casual observers the closeness of this mother-daughter relationship was admirable. But many pathological relationships appear innocent enough on the surface, and such was the case here. Patients often become overinvolved with parents who believe themselves to be thoughtful and interested. Such parents continually seek reassurance and demand regular phone calls, visits, and favors with little regard for the patient's neglect of his or her own life. The parents find a host of reasons for almost constant interaction. They pressure the patient to confide personal matters and to consult them on all decisions. Of course, they rationalize this intrusion as a willingness to help.

The parents of twenty-two-year-old Frances, for example, rationalized not letting go of their daughter because they feared that if they did "it would happen again." "It" was another suicide crisis. In fact, so obsessed was Frances's father with the possibility that he kept a file on her previous hospitalizations. This he insisted on reading out loud in my office—in Frances's presence.

Frances, who had had a strict Catholic upbringing, lived in her own apartment in Manhattan—an achievement in itself, considering her history. She held a job at which she was quite good. Being excessively conscientious, however, she gradually began to feel overwhelmed by her job, then guilty over being a "failure." All this time, her parents were continually phoning her to express their anxiety over her. This increased her sense of inadequacy—and her depression.

Finally, fearing another "episode," the family took her home, convinced her to stop working, and began doting on her. Like the family of the elderly businessman, they also pressured her to get out so she'd "feel better." These conflicting messages intensified her feelings of inadequacy, frustration, and guilt to the point where she took a knife to her throat.

Her mother stopped her and brought her to me.

Frances's parents were surprised by my attitude, which was to adopt a hands-off policy—to relax and *allow* her to feel depressed. I urged them to be supportive by being present, but not to push or be overprotective.

This was difficult for them to do. In fact, they were so preoccupied with their fear of another hospitalization that Frances could feel their anxiety. Actually, they felt more comfortable with her in the hospital than with their uncertainty over whether she would become ill again.

During treatment, Frances did have a relapse and required a brief hospitalization, but she is now doing much better, thanks in part to a less smothering, more hopeful attitude from her parents.

The lesson is that predictions of disaster often usher in the very disasters predicted. If you tell a person long enough that he or she is about to commit suicide, you should not be terribly surprised when the message finally sinks in and the individual makes the attempt.

Positive prophecies, on the other hand, can also be self-fulfilling. Try focusing on even the smallest bits of evidence that your depressed friend is improving, instead of focusing on the persistence of those symptoms that take longer to change. You may be surprised at the effect such a forward-looking input can have.

DO'S AND DON'T'S

While specific questions about how to behave toward the depressed or suicidal patient should be referred to the therapist, here is a summary of do's and don't's with which friends and relatives should be familiar.

DO'S

1. DO remove all weapons and potentially dangerous medications from the environment. Suicide attempts often occur impulsively and are beyond the individual's control. Therefore, many suicides could be prevented if the means were not available. *Remove all guns.* They account for approximately ten thousand deaths by suicide each year in the United States. *Remove poisons, barbiturates, and other potent drugs* as well. Barbiturates may alter consciousness, so that the individual may be unaware that he or she is taking a lethal overdose.

2. DO see that the patient takes the prescribed medicine. Remember that it takes some antidepressants several weeks to reach a therapeutic level in the bloodstream, so immediate relief from symptoms is rarely possible. Knowing that can make waiting easier for you and for the patient. During the initial stages of chemotherapy, the patient may experience such side effects as drowsiness, constipation, and dry mouth. Assure the patient that these usually disappear after a while.

3. DO discuss any doubts about the chemotherapy, or the treatment in general, with the therapist, *not* the patient. Expressions of doubt may undermine the patient's confidence in the treatment and retard his or her progress.

4. DO learn to recognize the early warning signs of depression and be aware of any changes in symptoms. If you notice an intensification of symptoms, contact the therapist or urge the patient to do so. Among the most common symptoms to watch for are sleep difficulties, preoccupation with sad thoughts, preoccupation with the disposition of possessions and unfinished business, poor appetite or compulsive overeating, loss of interest in one's surroundings and usual activities, loss of the ability to derive pleasure from

one's usual interests, loss of sexual desire, self-neglect, crying and tearfulness, loss of concentration and memory, hopelessness, suicidal thoughts or threats, feelings of persecution, and unexplainable euphoria or excitement. *Be especially alert to a sudden calm in a previously agitated person.*

5. DO remember that some people are ashamed of the idea of psychiatric illness. If you wish to advise someone to get treatment, the more you focus on the symptoms about which the individual is complaining (especially socially acceptable symptoms like low energy, insomnia, and tension headaches), the easier it will be. A blunt suggestion to go into intensive psychotherapy to get at the roots of the problem often produces resistance, while the suggestion that there is a specific medicine for relief of specific symptoms (as in the treatment of physical illness) is more readily accepted. *Important:* The person is usually not responsible for his or her symptoms and shouldn't be made to feel so.

6. DO know whom to call in case of an emergency. First, try to contact the suicide prevention clinic in your area, or the nearest hospital emergency room, or one of the local emergency services, which can be reached in many cities by dialing 911.

DON'T'S

1. DON'T undermine the patient's faith in the treatment by discussing your doubts or by recommending other doctors or clinics from which "miraculous" recoveries have been reported. While a second opinion can certainly help at the start, it may only confuse and trouble the patient after treatment has begun. Discuss these issues with the doctor first—*after* asking the patient's permission to do so.

2. DON'T become overinvolved in solving the patient's problems, and don't try out your own brand of therapy. Leave that to those with training.

3. DON'T push or prod the person to discuss his or her difficulties in an effort to understand their causes. Discussions of this nature are best left to the therapist. When the patient does offer to discuss his distress, a calm, listening attitude can be helpful.

4. DON'T make demands that might generate additional conflicts. Psychiatric patients often feel guilty and inadequate because reduced energy keeps them from pursuing their usual activities. Additional pressure only heightens their sense of being a "burden." It often takes a while before patients feel up to resuming their usual activities.

5. DON'T be impatient. The time needed for recovery varies with each individual. During this period it is best to be supportive and sympathetic.

6. DON'T assume the patient's responsibilities. Excessive helpfulness can burden both the patient and you, and generates mutual resentment. It's better to help patients to help themselves than to do things for them that they can do on their own. That way you help to bolster their self-confidence and courage to live.

7

The Crisis

Seek, seek for him!
Lest his ungovern'd rage dissolve the life
That wants the means to lead it.
—WILLIAM SHAKESPEARE,
King Lear, act 4, scene 4

Suicidal crises always seem to occur before holidays and long weekends. People get fired on Friday, or they get "discharged" from work until the following Monday, which makes over sixty hours to go before they're *needed* again. For the lonely and depressed, the weekend waits like a fearsome, shapeless specter.

I can't tell you how often I have been confronted by a crisis on a Friday afternoon. A suicide attempt has been made; anxious relatives want the patient hospitalized immediately. Either the patient refuses hospitalization or no free beds can be found. As a result, one must face the long weekend with little certainty as to whether the patient will make another attempt.

Repeated attempts happen most often in the first weeks and months following an initial attempt. For this reason, especially careful observation of the patient is in order immediately following a suicide attempt. And this includes, strangely enough, observation even while the patient is hospitalized. Indeed, a near-suicide who is hospitalized often proves to be a particularly dangerous risk. Many hospitals, unacquainted with a patient's history of depression, tend to treat "failed" suicides as only temporary risks; once they understand the immediate external stresses or personality weakness that led to the episode, they are content to deal with the symptoms of the depression and relax their general vigilance.

Sometimes this is a fatal mistake. In our studies of suicidal patients, both at the crisis intervention clinic at the Payne Whitney Clinic of New York Hospital and at the Social Psychiatry Research Institute, we found that an alarmingly large percentage of patients attempted suicide while under medical care. Some patients who appeared calm and cooperative on the surface actually killed themselves while *in* a hospital.

Therefore, it is of paramount importance that friends as well as physicians be alert to the moods of patients who have recently been "saved" from suicide, lest they find that the salvation is only temporary.

We also found that mildly and moderately disturbed patients were a *greater* risk of suicide than the severely depressed or schizophrenic who were likely to be referred to a hospital or psychiatrist. This somewhat surprising discovery points to an interesting factor to consider when attempting to predict who will commit, or attempt to commit, suicide—and when. It is not always the most obviously depressed people who are the likely candidates for suicide. On the contrary, those to watch out for are often the patients who show a sudden or uncustomary sense of contentment after a period of marked depression. They exhibit not radically disturbed behavior, but what I would call an ominous calm, like the calm before a storm.

THE OMINOUS CALM

Let us assume that someone you know exhibits typical presuicidal behavior, including expressions of futility and hopelessness, and references to suicide; expressions of the inability to meet the demands of friends and relatives; threats of suicide in the context of considerable conflict with others; actions that increase conflict and result in friends' and relatives' attempts to control the individual; expressions of anxiety; behavior that is passive and manipulative; or an unwillingness to accept the fact that he or she has a definable illness that can be treated.

Now let us suppose that your friend, who has been exhibiting these characteristics for some time, suddenly becomes quite calm, quite self-assured. His or her complaints about life miraculously vanish, and a new resoluteness appears. The individual becomes inexplicably generous, giving away some prized possessions. All in all, he or she displays a serenity you have not seen for years.

How should you interpret this behavior?

Most of us would rejoice in such a transformation. That would be a mistake, perhaps a deadly mistake. For the change I have just described is typical, paradoxically, not of patients who are actually (as well as visibly) improving, but of patients who are actually on the brink of a serious attempt to end their lives. The resoluteness, the apparent serenity, even the ritualistic surrender to friends of their worldly goods—all are facets of a new and fatal determination. Such behavior, which looks so confident on the surface, often disguises a grim sense of purpose. Persons exhibiting such behavior should be watched very carefully, for they are entering a dangerous time.

Another dangerous time is that immediately following a suicide attempt. Often at this time an individual seems much better and less depressed than usual, and, tragically, many friends and relatives take this as evidence that the patient got what he or she wanted out of the attempt: the sympathy of those around him or her. "Sure he's feeling fine," they say. "Everybody's fawning over him."

Again, this can be a major error. Whatever the popular conceptions of suicide, no one attempts it merely as a bid for sympathy. Shrugging off suicide attempts as bids for attention is an irresponsible interpretation which, unfortunately, probably accounts for the rapidity with which many hospitals discharge seriously disturbed patients after they have dealt with the immediate causes of their depressions and sewn up their self-inflicted wounds.

Voiced concern about one's condition, then, can actually be an encouraging sign. A severely depressed person who ceases to complain about feeling miserable may simply have given up and decided coolly and firmly to put an end to his or her suffering. This is not to say that a constant complainer is in a healthy state, but at least the individual may not be on the verge of an irretrievable action.

This is borne out by the results of our investigations. We interviewed a large sample of patients, first at the time of their suicide attempts and then one year later. The results indicated that expressions of distress over their symptoms were usually a favorable sign. Such expressions occurred with greater frequency among the group that showed definite improvement in a year's time (43 percent), while those who subsequently died from a repeat attempt (2.7 percent) were least likely to have expressed distress or created much interpersonal conflict.

Beware the ominous calm. It can be a telltale sign of impending disaster.

THE CRISIS CALL

You are sleeping late on a Saturday morning when the telephone rings. Blearily, you pick up the receiver and recognize the voice of a friend you had been having drinks with the night before. There is something different in his voice, a note of flat urgency at odds with the hail-fellow-well-met attitude he had displayed several hours earlier. And then you hear what he is saying, and you are suddenly wide awake.

"I just wanted somebody to know. I've had it. Had enough. Just wanted you to know, that's all."

As you realize he is talking about killing himself, you are dumbstruck. Not only does it come as a complete surprise to you, but you feel thoroughly unprepared to deal with the situation, afraid that anything you say may be the wrong thing, may push him over the edge.

You realize you should keep him on the phone, talk him out of it. But what can you say?

Fortunately, this is a situation few people are likely ever to be confronted with. But such calls—to friends, to therapists, to family—happen all the time. About a year ago, I received such a call from a middle-aged former patient. Her voice was drained of emotion as she recited the litany of her failings. Then she confessed why she'd called:

"I'm giving up. I've been defeated my whole life. . . . Right now, I have a very hollow feeling. I have an intense desire to go to an all-night drugstore and buy a razor blade and bleed to death. I have nothing left . . . no friends. . . . There's nothing in this world I want except death."

This woman, a profoundly disturbed divorcée, was shackled by an impossible family situation full of hostile, rejecting relatives, and was an extremely high suicide risk. I realized at once that this was no bid for attention, and decided to force her to focus on the potentials still left in her shattered life. "You'd be surprised what you have left if you can just get in touch with it," I told her, reminding her that she did, in fact, possess many qualities and talents. She depreciated those talents, but I kept coming back to them, insisting that *something* could still be salvaged. Gradually her denials abated, and she calmed down sufficiently to agree to reenter treatment. Like many crisis calls, this one lasted for hours.

Anyone who receives a suicide crisis call should be aware first of the varied impulses that may have prompted it. The caller may simply need to reach out to a concerned, caring voice in a hostile world, or need to ventilate his or her feelings. Some crisis callers use the person at the other end of the line as a verbal punching bag, displacing the hostility they feel for somebody else. Some disturbed people, for example, call suicide prevention clinics or "hot lines" deliberately to bait or insult the listener as a kind of revenge against another professional—usually a therapist—who is or was treating them.

There are basic techniques for handling such calls, techniques used by most suicide prevention clinics around the country. It is useful to understand them in the event that you answer the phone one day and hear: "I have nothing to live for. I'm going to kill myself."

HANDLING THE CRISIS CALL

First of all, make the caller aware that there is professional help available, and encourage him or her to seek it. If you encounter resistance or apathy, and if you sense that it might be dangerous to hang up, *keep the person talking* and remember these precepts:

1. *Don't panic.* Talk calmly and reasonably.

2. *Keep the lines of communication open.* The caller wanted someone to talk to and needs to know that you understand how he or she feels.

3. *Focus on the problem.* Don't get sidetracked by a discussion of symptoms or irrelevant matters. Find out what precipitated the crisis. Try to get the caller to externalize the problem by putting it into realistic perspective.

4. *Identify the loss.* Was the precipitating event the loss of a spouse, friend, job, position, status, or what? Empathize, but try to put the loss into realistic perspective.

5. *Latch on to the will to live.* Remember, a potential suicide is ambivalent; *part of the individual doesn't want to die.* Something the caller says will most likely give you the

opportunity to recognize it and point out that "part of you wants to live."

6. **Don't get into a debate.** Don't argue the merits of life versus suicide. In particular, don't get trapped into answering a question like "Give me one good reason why I should go on living." Any answer you can give to such a question will be shot down. Avoid platitudes like "Life is so wonderful" or "You have everything to live for." These comments, well-meant as they may be, will only convince the caller that you don't really understand how he or she feels.

7. **Be supportive.** Look for the person's positive, attractive qualities and previous successes, however small, in order to evoke his or her awareness of alternatives.

8. **Suggest feasible options.** Suggest some objective that can be pursued, or a task that can easily be accomplished, to break the cycle of defeat and provide an avenue for achievement and a sense of mastery over the situation.

9. **Don't give direct advice.** Encourage the caller to make his or her own choices.

You can help to alleviate the caller's distress by defusing the crisis and helping the individual to gain an understanding of the situation which may reorient him or her to the precrisis level of functioning. Then, once you have assisted the caller to calm down, you should recommend that he or she seek professional help.

CRISIS INTERVENTION°

Most people who attempt suicide have ambivalent motivations about it. Therefore, it's nearly impossible to determine

---

° For further information about suicide prevention programs in your area, contact the local medical society, your family physician, a regional medical school, or write to: The Social Psychiatry Research Institute, Lenox Hill Station, 219 East 70th Street, P.O. Box 605, New York, N.Y. 10021.

who is most likely to "go through with it." However, high-risk depressed patients tend to fall into four categories:

1. Middle-aged males recently separated from their wives and/or unemployed.
2. Alcoholic females.
3. Young drug abusers.
4. The isolated elderly.

For men, the suicidal crisis most often relates to their work experience. This occurs particularly in their late forties and fifties, when they feel they no longer have the same energy or opportunities as before. By contrast, suicidal women more often report failures in personal relationships.

While these general categories of high-risk people make it easier to formulate general expectations of the likelihood of suicide, they do not really help us to construct individual treatments. For this, personal investigation of the individual crisis is essential, as is focusing on the specific symptoms involved. Both at Cornell and at the Social Psychiatry Research Institute, I have found the most effective method of crisis intervention to be this kind of symptom-directed treatment—an approach designed first to relieve the present distress and then to prevent further crises.

Patients receive instructions regarding the nature of their condition, the role of medication, the possibility of side effects, and the procedures to follow in case of emergency or heightened conflict.

With supportive psychotherapy, patients learn to *stop doing what they don't want to do* and, as rapidly as possible, *shift to hitherto untapped areas of strength.*

In a crisis intervention clinic, treatment generally proceeds through the following stages:

STAGE I: DEALING WITH THE IMMEDIATE CRISIS

Initially, treatment focuses on a review of symptoms and interpersonal problems that may have triggered the suicidal crisis. With progress, attention focuses on encouraging a healthy self-interest and a reevaluation of existing relationships. Patients learn to *relinquish responsibility for symptoms* such as insomnia, loss of appetite, and loss of energy, which result from the depression, but to *accept responsibility for their actions*—for instance, for help and relating to others.

STAGE II: REEDUCATION

Strengthening self-reliance and the capacity to cope with stress can help to develop alternative ways of functioning. Through anticipation and planning for difficult situations, we may prevent stress, reduce overreaction, and increase satisfaction and a sense of security. Assets, strengths, and liabilities can then be redefined and appropriate personal goals established.

STAGE III: TAKING CONTROL OF YOUR LIFE

Psychotherapy serves as a catalyst to bring about significant change. This is achieved through the encouragement of experimentation with new ways of behaving in real-life situations.

Treatment moves most rapidly when the patient focuses on concrete, everyday situations that offer the greatest opportunity for testing new ways of behaving. This process involves learning to do what makes most sense in terms of natural abilities, and learning to say no to requests that the patient finds burdensome or would assume only out of a sense of obligation.

It takes time and effort for attitudes and relationships to

change. Don't expect to overcome lifelong habits merely by acknowledging them as habits. Change takes practice. Each day offers countless opportunities for discovering that you can take charge of your life in the direction of your choice.

STAGE IV: A WORTHY PURPOSE

A variety of changes in patients' lives often occurs prior to or following a suicide attempt. Some face custody fights, divorce proceedings, or unemployment. Others encounter prejudice and feel stigmatized. However, these adversities offer opportunities to establish a meaningful objective or worthy purpose.

Focusing on a long-range objective makes it easier to move through stressful situations. As the German therapist Victor Frankl observed about his fellow survivors of the Nazi death camps, "If you have a *why* to live, you can endure almost any *how*."

The period after a suicide attempt can be especially stressful if the attempt was precipitated by the loss of a loved one. This is particularly true for very dependent individuals who are not challenged by new circumstances to become independent and self-reliant. The elderly often need the assistance of social services, particularly when their lives have been built around a spouse. Serious physical illness and fewer social roles at this age level further reduce flexibility and adaptability and contribute to suicidal risk.

Often the patient's behavior subsequent to a suicide attempt intensifies social stress and keeps the patient a high risk. Some feel compelled to confess excessively to others in an effort to make amends for supposed past wrongdoing. Others fail to pursue their own interests. Many get involved in complicated relationships or resort to alcohol and drugs. Many undergo major personality changes, which can create new pressures and precipitate new crises. Relatives and friends sometimes withdraw, allowing others to take responsibility for the patient's welfare, and the patient may interpret this as rejection.

The therapist must keep all such potential difficulties in mind while insisting that the patient concentrate on the purpose he or she has chosen. Often a determined, almost meditative single-mindedness at this time is an effective antidote to the inevitable confusion that results from reorganizing one's life.

STAGE V: MANAGING YOUR TIME

The healthiest among us do not have the time to do everything. Once a suicidal crisis is averted, therefore, it's important that the patient remember his or her limits as well as the expanded possibilities. Some recovering patients have the feeling that whereas before they could do nothing, now they must do it all. This can be counterproductive, for overextension after a crisis could easily lead to disappointment and bring on renewed feelings of frustration. We counsel our patients to use their time judiciously, to adopt strategies for conserving their resources and *maximizing the potential of the moment.*

To maximize the moment, you should weigh the time you spend in particular activities or relationships against your overall priorities. Efficient time management can help you overcome obstacles and initiate activities that bring immediate results. By setting challenging but *attainable* goals, you can achieve the greatest satisfaction, thereby reinforcing your courage to live.

Sympathetic counseling here can ensure that a recovering patient not spread newly liberated energies too thinly. This in turn can ensure a growing sense of satisfaction, as the patient comes to enjoy the advantages of a responsibly, rather than a neurotically, organized life.

8

Self-Destructing Slowly

And she is dying piece-meal
of a sort of emotional anaemia.
                —Ezra Pound, "The Garden"

You need not put a gun to your head or a knife to your wrists to be self-destructive.

Suicides, in fact, comprise a relatively small proportion of the people who are destroying themselves throughout the world each day. The majority of cases of self-destruction are more subtle than actual suicide. I spoke earlier of these cases of "mini-suicide"; in this chapter I want to look at some of the ways in which people eat away at their self-respect and effectiveness, and try to show how such insidiously masochistic behavior might be avoided.

Actually, cases of slow self-destruction may in the long run be just as damaging to the individual as cases of out-and-out, despair-induced suicide. For the effect is nearly the same: to deprive the individual of the opportunity to conduct a full and productive life. And since identifying such behavior is much harder than identifying clearly suicidal behavior, it may end up lasting longer and thereby taking more out of the person involved.

In Chapter 6 I spoke of the need for suicidal patients to maximize their opportunities by concentrating on projects that are important to them and avoiding activities that deflect them from these pursuits. Those who self-destruct slowly are, in a way, doing just the opposite of that. They are allowing their available energies to be sapped in inefficient pursuits, while what really interests them goes begging.

What are some of the ways in which people allow themselves to be worn down in this way? And do you yourself engage in such self-defeating behavior?

Most of us commit small acts of "suicide" every day. Ask yourself, for example, whether or not you do any of the following:

1. Arrive late or improperly dressed for business meetings.

2. Provoke arguments with those you care about.

3. Fail to study for important examinations.

4. Stuff yourself with junk food, knowing its nutritional value is low.

5. Ignore the surgeon general's warning about smoking.

6. Simply squander your talents by not *using* them.

If you do engage in these sorts of behaviors, you probably also have many rationalizations to explain them away. You don't like to be tied down by convention; you cannot help getting into an argument if someone annoys you; "last-minute" studying doesn't do any good; there's nothing wrong with eating food you enjoy; smoking doesn't affect *your* health; you don't want to get caught up in our competitive, materialistic society.

Many people create their own failures and suffering because they are afraid of pursuing their own objectives wholeheartedly. Some people actually fear success more than they do failure, and to ensure that they will not have to contend with the added responsibilities of success, they court disappointment, telling themselves when they fail that it's "not worth the trouble anyway." By committing themselves to their objectives only partially, they frequently turn their expectation of failure into reality. Here again is a sadly self-fulfilling prophecy.

Other people focus too much attention on results and look for shortcuts to success. They refuse to apply the *persistent* effort that must be employed in order to reach goals, and convince themselves that their meager efforts really constituted a "good try."

Consider. Do any of the following questions apply to you?

1. Do you dwell on what is probably unattainable?

2. Do you focus excessive criticism on yourself, thereby undermining your self-confidence?

3. Are you preoccupied with the past or the future, ignoring opportunities in the present?

4. Do you dwell on problems instead of creating solutions?

5. Do you seek the opinions of others in areas where you already know the answers?

If the answers are yes, perhaps you can now account for certain vague, unexplained feelings of guilt and inadequacy you've experienced. To compensate for these unpleasant feelings, you may have assumed others' problems and responsibilities, which, instead of making you feel better, made you feel more frustrated and angry. Usually such an accumulation of unpleasant feelings sabotages productive efforts toward self-fulfillment and leads to more serious forms of self-defeating behavior and depression.

In the remainder of this chapter I want to focus on some of the common ways in which self-destruction is manifested in our society. The first way is perhaps the most ironic one: a driving commitment to success which, because the people who engage in it overextend themselves, inevitably leads to failure.

SELF-DESTRUCTIVE PATTERNS OF "SUCCESS"

People who are very anxious or compulsively driven to "succeed" often become self-destructive in the process. The greater their efforts to function at a high level, the more self-destructive they become.

In the past several years, a number of successful physicians have consulted me because of their increasing dependence upon a variety of sedative and stimulant drugs—chiefly barbiturates to help them to sleep, and amphetamines to give them the energy to maintain their tremendous pace of activities.

The need for larger and larger doses to produce the same effects resulted in a cycle of dependence habituation and progressively more severe withdrawal symptoms. By the time they consulted me, this syndrome had begun to impair their work and jeopardize their careers, until under pressure from families and colleagues they sought treatment to help them withdraw from these drugs.

Now, while it may seem curious that professional people in a position of community responsibility should fall prey to such a self-destructive habit, in fact this kind of drug abuse is not uncommon among people in high-pressure occupations, and especially in those where there is ready access to medication. These doctors' drug abuse began, in fact, as unmonitored self-medication, and only gradually developed into a problematic dependence. I began treating them with a combination of antidepressant and antianxiety medication. Subsequent psychotherapy revealed that the common denominator motivating these men had been an overriding ambition to succeed and a marked inability to pace themselves.

Perhaps it is not surprising, then, that they should have turned to barbiturates. Their self-imposed heavy work load created anxiety; the anxiety made them sleepless, at night as well as during the day; and sedatives were the obvious solution.

The same kind of pattern of abuse is often found among hard-driving executives in the business world. Their pressured life-style makes many of them turn not to drugs but to the most readily available addictive substance in our society: alcohol. In the next sections I will examine the problem of alcohol abuse, which is certainly the widest example in twentieth-century America of slow, socially acceptable suicide.

ALCOHOL ABUSE

The link between alcohol abuse and self-destruction is sometimes difficult to establish in a society that makes alcohol available almost everywhere—in restaurants, theaters, airplanes, commuter trains, and even, in some states, supermarkets and drugstores. Drinking in this country connotes sociability, freedom, and the "good life."

Drinking also plays an important symbolic role in rites of passage—birth, confirmation, marriage, anniversaries, retirement. Let someone get hired, fired, promoted, divorced, or honored; let him win a game, a raffle, or a bet—and it becomes an occasion for the invitation "Let's have a drink."

In moderation, alcohol can have a beneficial effect. A drink "breaks the ice" at social gatherings. It can help you unwind after a hectic day. And no one would deny that an occasional bout of tipsiness, of "loosening up," provides, in our high-pressure society, a healthy antidote to the constant daily grind.

But what do we mean by "occasional"?

Of course, everyone's body chemistry is different, and what would be excessive for one person might barely affect another. In general, however, what you should be on the outlook for, with alcohol as with any other addictive substance, is *regular,* continued use. It is when alcohol consumption evolves into a habitual routine that it is on the way to becoming a problem.

If, for example, you drink on a *daily* basis—no matter how little—you should consider that you may at some time in the future be at risk as a habitual drinker. This is not to suggest that all daily drinkers eventually cease to be able to hold their liquor, or that a person who drinks a six-pack a day is destined to develop cirrhosis of the liver or other alcohol-related health problems. Nothing is that certain, but my warning is based on a simple and easily verifiable fact:

Alcohol is an addictive substance.

This means that progressive use of the substance leads to addiction. The hard drinker eventually will have to drink more to achieve the same effect because the body will build up a tolerance to the initial amount. As with sedatives, then, the dosage tends inevitably to rise. And ultimately the body learns to rely on the drug to the extent that cessation of use can lead to withdrawal symptoms. These symptoms may be nothing so blatant or colorful as the notorious delirium tremens; they may consist only of a vague edginess, a mild irritability, or the half-conscious yearning for "just one beer to whet my whistle." Not anything shocking, but enough to be concerned about. For they are indications of at least a psychological, and probably a physical, dependency.

Alcohol reduces anxiety, but it also dulls the senses and warps judgment. Furthermore, as the use of it grows, so do physiological problems. Appetite and enthusiasm, for example, may decline. Sleep may be restless and troubled. Irritability and depression may ensue, reinforcing the urge to drink more. This can catapult the drinker into a no-win addictive cycle: the more you drink to alleviate depression, the more depressed you become—and the more you must drink to compensate.

Consider the case of Paul, an industrial designer in his fifties who was devastated by the combination of a divorce and severe financial reversals. Lonely and anxious, distraught over losing custody of his two teenage sons, Paul turned to drink for relief but only became progressively more withdrawn and alienated.

Physical symptoms plagued him: headaches, dizziness, an inability to sleep, chest pains, and a vague, gnawing sensation at the pit of his stomach. Unable to work efficiently, indecisive and forgetful, he made numerous critical mistakes at work and eventually was fired.

Guilty and ashamed of his drastic decline, he drank more and became preoccupied with suicidal ideas. When he found himself making specific plans, he became frightened and sought medical help. Treatment focused on stopping all drinking, taking antidepressant medication for the relief of symptoms, and finally thoroughly reviewing his life situation with a view toward reducing his stress and redirecting his energy into more rewarding directions.

As Paul improved he assumed more responsibility for his life and began to fashion a plan of action designed to minimize the stresses caused by too many commitments. As often happens, treatment provided the impetus for him to resume some activities that he had previously avoided or neglected, and he became stronger than before. In fact, he developed enough confidence in himself to start his own business—fulfilling a lifelong dream—which he has since pursued with success.

SOLVING A DRINKING PROBLEM

Rarely are people able to stop drinking by a single act of willpower. Social pressures often make it difficult. Many people find it awkward, for instance, to say no when pressured to "have just one drink."

If someone close to you drinks heavily, remember that you aren't helping if you attack that person on moral grounds or inquire repeatedly, "Haven't you had enough?" Nagging only accentuates anxiety and guilt. The more you accuse, the more you reinforce a problem drinker's inclination to find rapid relief in alcohol.

Resisting the urge to nag and criticize isn't easy. It requires patience and self-control, particularly since alcoholics are destructive not only of themselves but of those around them, and particularly those they love.

If you are an alcoholic, you in turn must resist the inclination to indulge in guilt and remorse by listening to such criticism. Even well-intentioned criticism can intensify your anxiety and guilt, and provide you with an incentive for drinking again. If you let this happen, you are making others responsible for your drinking, and reducing your inclination to take control of your life.

As a first step in curtailing a drinking problem, you must consider which situations in your daily life might be forcing you to drink, and which you can deal with differently. Determine some of the ways in which you may have given up responsibility for yourself. Pinpoint the *specific situations* in which you feel pressured to drink; you may make a start in controlling your urge to drink simply by avoiding those situations.

Most important of all, *learn how to turn down a drink.*

Social pressure and personal habit conspire to make this apparently simple procedure one of the hardest things a steady drinker has to learn. There is, however, at least one simple trick you can employ at, say, a party where everyone is expected to indulge. A friend of mine, formerly a heavy drinker, utilizes this tactic regularly to good effect.

Immediately upon entering the party, instead of shying away from the bar, he goes right up to it and orders a tall glass of ice water. This he carries around with him, sipping at it periodically; so far, he says, no one has ever assumed he is drinking anything but vodka. The tactic saves him the embarrassment of explaining himself to other guests, and saves the host and hostess the burden of going out of their way to load down the poor man "on the wagon" with hors d'oeuvres and other consolations.

Self-examination is also a valuable aspect of learning to stop drinking. You might try asking yourself: How can I make tomorrow different? How can I avoid some of the pressures I am likely to encounter?

Remember that it is the accumulation of small pressures that creates the greatest stress for most people. If, on occasion, the accumulation of stress leads you to question the value of your medicine and/or psychotherapy, you may be tempted to have a drink. You must learn to resist such temptation, understanding that drinking can only aggravate the stress.

Shaking a drinking habit takes time. It takes time to adopt new patterns of living to reduce the stress in your life. But by modifying small bits of your behavior, you *will* be able to change. You won't lose your "identity" in the process but will have the opportunity to become true to the valuable person you really are.

RISKING SELF-DESTRUCTION

Depressed individuals often court self-destruction through high-risk activity. Consciously or unconsciously, they are seeking relief from their depression through the "high-risk high."

During high-risk activity, your blood pressure soars, your pulse rate accelerates, and your heart pounds as adrenaline discharges into your bloodstream. Such brief bursts of adrenaline give you a chance to tap normally unrealized strengths and may produce a feeling of great excitement.

Many depressed individuals enter into risk-taking activity with these physiological and psychological responses in mind. Too often, however, they do so without the training and preparation that professional risk-takers—such as athletes, test pilots, and stunt men—undergo. This lack of preparation increases the risk, naturally, but may also intensify the high.

For certain depressed individuals, mastering their responses to danger or challenges makes them feel better about themselves. Risk-taking for them serves as an antidote to apathy and inadequacy. It gives them a lift—but at a price, and only temporarily.

Sometimes such risk-taking can appear quite beneficial. Forced to get themselves in at least temporary physical shape to meet a dangerous test, some normally depressed individuals have been known to go off alcohol, for example, in order to improve their chances of successfully meeting the test. While this is a clear case of robbing Peter to pay Paul, at least it has a salutary side effect.

A fine balance between self-destructiveness and self-actualization may even develop in these cases. From the experience of mastering a tricky physical situation, some depressed people learn that it is their behavior and skill—not merely chance—that determines the outcome of their lives and ultimately how they feel about themselves. This can have a positive effect on their images of themselves. So perhaps in some cases courting risk is a not unworthy price to pay for an enhancement of self-esteem.

While I would not think of counseling a depressed person to, say, sky-dive as a means of therapy, I must admit that, in the final analysis, the balance between self-mastery and disaster often heightens the individual's sense of life and produces a high. If you happen to be *mildly* depressed, this experience *may* give you a sufficient sense of exhilaration and self-confidence to propel you out of your depressed state and your passive-dependent ways of relating to others.

In some cases, however, the depressed person is really only courting death—only "trying out" suicide in a socially acceptable guise. He or she, in trying to experience the high associated with mastery of a difficult physical task, may escalate the risk without increasing the necessary preparation for meeting that risk intelligently. Instead of methodically engaging in such activities in a planned, step-by-step manner, he or she may merely act impulsively, thereby substantially increasing the chances of tragedy.

Now, while this kind of behavior often ensures the person an immediate intensification of the high, in the long run it is really not a very good method of learning to accept oneself as masterful. By heightening the danger beyond reasonable limits, the individual may actually set up a situation where he or she experiences more stress than elation—and in such a situation, of course, the whole point of the exercise is lost.

This happened to Leonora.

To look at Leonora, you would never dream that she might be depressed. Following her divorce, she seemed quite happy about having the freedom to do as she pleased. A glamorous model and darling of the jet set, she spoke several languages, traveled widely, and met many interesting people.

She found, however, that she was fighting an unpleasant sense of boredom.

To alleviate it, Leonora constantly sought new thrills: big-game hunting in Africa; scuba diving in Barbados; skiing in Kitzbühel, parachute jumping in Connecticut, riding the surf in California. Nothing satisfied her, not the yachts of the superrich nor her athletic achievements—which she began to push to fairly dangerous limits. The adrenaline-generated excitement never lasted very long before her boredom and depression returned.

Eventually, her risk-taking assumed such self-destructive dimensions that she seemed hell-bent on destroying herself. Fortunately, friends persuaded her to enter treatment before this happened.

Antidepressant medications proved helpful in alleviating Leonora's tension and frustration. Simultaneously, efforts were made through discussions to get her to see how much she had been functioning in terms of her public image. Leonora had never comprehended the degree to which she had been pressured to live up to her reputation as a "swinger" who would try anything once.

Moreover, she had never been aware of how much she had ignored her real interests: writing and languages. She had avoided them as too "intellectual"—that is, contrary to the live-wire image she had projected. With encouragement to do what she genuinely *wanted* to do, she resumed her study of Romance languages and began to write poetry. Within a year she had translated and published a small book of Italian poetry.

Much of the thrust of Leonora's treatment was to make her realize that she was under no compulsion to participate in any activity either to impress others or to alleviate boredom, and that her true identity lay in conducting her life as *she* wished.

THE DRIFTERS

A final, and especially troublesome, type of self-destruction is characterized by a type of behavior that might be seen as the reverse of Leonora's. Whereas she grasped at an excess of life in the hope of finding one morsel that would satisfy her, some depressed people take the opposite tack and refuse to grasp at anything at all. For them, life becomes an untouched banquet, a parade that passes by.

Apathy, that gray brooding ghost that collars each of us from time to time, seizes these people with a forcefulness that belies its name. Beginning with a timidity about doing things that might expose them to ridicule or rejection, they gradually drift into a condition of constant ennui, unable to marshal the energies for anything at all. Everything becomes a potential threat. Nothing is interesting enough to try. They are too weary today; it's too sunny tomorrow, or too gray. Every day finds its own excuse for retirement until, without knowing how it has happened, they have drifted into permanent disinterest, as emotional invalids unable to respond to anything but food, television, and sleep.

Such people are among the saddest and at the same time most aggravating individuals anyone is likely to encounter. Treatment is difficult because it involves, first of all, bringing the depressed person to the realization that he or she is in fact depressed. So far from the normal channels of communication do some of these drifters allow themselves to get that the physician is often at a loss to make the necessary initial contacts.

In situations like this, the assistance of significant others can be quite valuable, for generally the last linkages to normal social intercourse are those to family and friends, and while they may be ineffective in solving such withdrawal problems, they can be quite useful in pointing out the existence of the dilemma.

Paradoxically, people in such an empty, disinterested position might have readier access to help if they were so depressed that they were actively considering suicide. Crisis demands assistance; boredom does not. It is terribly difficult for a person without interests—without even a vivid, discernible depression—to be reached by conventional means.

How do we save these walking dead? Patience, first of all. Patience—and perhaps an uncustomary insistence. Provided that suicide is not an imminent threat, a forceful insistence in such cases that the person take a serious look at himself or herself might be more effective—and is certainly more appropriate—than a willingness to go along with the individual's bland avowal that "nothing is wrong."

Sometimes the depressed must be forced to be free. Measuring when to be accommodating and when to be adamant is never easy, for the professional or for the layperson. But for those who have drifted into this kind of fondly cherished sloth, adamancy may be the shock they need to open their eyes to the issue.

No one, I believe, should simply be permitted to kill himself or herself, quickly or slowly, by depression. For those who are drifting without knowing it, a timely yell may be in order. Not a reprimand. Just the observation "Hey, look where you're going."

9

What Have You Got to Lose?

For this is the journey that men make to find themselves.
—JAMES MICHENER, *The Fires of Spring*

In these days of recurrent energy crises, we often overlook one of the most widespread of such crises: the one that exists in the lives of those who never discover or never utilize the enormous potential within themselves. Not only the depressed but many among us stand like spectators of our own lives, neglecting to tap the forces at our fingertips. We are like a man stranded at an oasis in the desert who merely stares at the water flowing from a spring and, out of perversity or boredom or habit, will not drink.

We all, like the bad servant in the parable, waste our talents. Perhaps the most reckless squanderers of their energy are those who attempt suicide, but few of us can be called really frugal or resourceful when it comes to managing the potentials within. Sleepwalking through our lives, we miss countless opportunities for fruitful activity and growth, often simply because we are afraid to take the chance needed to seize them. In this chapter I want to suggest some of the reasons that so many of us waste our potential, and indicate a general approach to our life opportunities that would minimize this waste. Only by recognizing that we do indeed hold our lives in our own hands can we take advantage of the daily opportunities for self-enrichment; doing so can make our brief sojourn on this planet more productive, more healthful, and happier.

SETTING OUT

Imagine you are that man in the oasis. Wary of drinking from an unknown spring, you are nevertheless eventually forced to do so because you realize that you will otherwise die of thirst. But having done that, you are again stymied. Sands surround you on every side. You know that somewhere beyond their undulating emptiness lies food and shelter and human companionship. But you are afraid to set out to find them.

So eventually you expire there in the oasis, miles from any human contact. True, you might have perished on the journey, had you undertaken it. But in the oasis, comfortably, you simply starve.

A fanciful analogy? Not so fanciful, really. For many of us are in the condition of such a man in the desert. We are perfectly well aware that remaining where we are—caught, that is, in our habitual neurotic patterns—will ensure that we will die without ever having tackled our own best selves. Yet we stay circling in those patterns, anyway—simply because we prefer a known emptiness to an unknown anything else.

Fear breeds inertia, rigidity, sameness; few other human attitudes have limited and thwarted so many human lives as the attitude of "playing it safe."

Fear of economic disaster, for example, can lock you into a stressful and boring work situation.

Fear of criticism or failure can inhibit your thinking and acting, and foster feelings of helplessness, resentment, and frustration.

Fear of bad luck in love can mean you will never reach out, will never know love at all.

Anticipating the worst, you may spend most of your energy trying to control your natural inclinations. If you avoid speaking up or making decisions or trying something new, your true abilities may never be developed or expressed.

Yet taking risks characterizes the best in all human endeavor. It makes possible innovation, change, and growth, and it is the field for the development of the richest human qualities, including courage, imagination, and joy.

I do not mean, of course, that you should rush headlong into blatantly dangerous or compromising situations. That is the way of the neurotic individual who, like Leonora in Chapter 8, must continually test himself or herself in order to bolster an essentially pessimistic view of personal potential. There is a difference between recklessness and intelligent risk, between positive and negative risk-taking. The person who profits from taking risks takes them not to court death or danger for its own sake but because placing oneself in a difficult, challenging situation brings out the best in one, generates hitherto untapped resources. And the individual does this in a planned, deliberate manner.

In other words, the elements of uncertainty and risk involved in change can be tempered with knowledge and preparation. This is dramatically illustrated in certain occupations.

Astronauts, coal miners, auto racers, skiers, and many circus performers, for example, regularly travel along the cutting edge of life.

Their basic approach to developing their abilities is to begin at the level of least challenge and, as their skills improve, steadily escalate the challenge. Their increasing preparedness and training minimize the risk of failure—or disaster.

Those whose vocation or avocation entails a fair degree of risk frequently report feeling most alive when their fate hangs in the balance. A European high-wire artist has talked of feeling "totally alive" when his act involves the most risk, as if in walking a tight wire he fully controls his own destiny.

Through total concentration on the task at hand and the exclusion of extraneous thoughts, such individuals virtually banish anxiety, often reaching a state of tremendous internal satisfaction (the natural adrenaline high referred to in Chapter 8).

But the risk need not be life-threatening for you to experience a high. All change involves risk, and the sense of accomplishment that comes from making a change for which you have carefully prepared yourself can lead to your discovering new ways of functioning in other areas of your life.

The important thing is to begin, to step away from the oasis and make the attempt to discover new territory before the voracious sense of inertia takes over and you find yourself running the same treadmill at the end of your life as you were running when you were a child.

But how do you begin? How do you set out on that journey to yourself?

While no one can do more than point the general direction for another person, there are certain basic guidelines that you may find helpful. Before you can expect to accomplish anything successfully, you must at the very least:

1. Set yourself a definite goal.
2. Be prepared to assess your progress periodically.
3. Ignore the "insights" of others who serve as mentors, rivals, or gadflies.

SETTING GOALS

You can learn to take intelligent risks by acting in a self-assertive way. Setting goals for yourself will help you to do this.

A goal is a powerful motivating force. It can help you

overcome a fear of being rejected or abandoned. It can mobilize your energies and direct them in an effective way. Moreover, in the pursuit of a meaningful goal you will learn things about yourself that you never knew.

It's of relatively little importance what kind of goal you set for yourself, as long as it is not so unrealistic that shooting for it is sure to invite disappointment and frustration. Some formerly depressed patients of mine have learned new languages, picked up a musical instrument, or simply determined to get themselves a job they liked. It is not necessary to climb Mount Everest or swim the English Channel in order to generate your positive energies. Pick something you really *want* to do, not something that would merely look impressive in a biography.

And don't worry too much about failing. Setbacks are inevitable, but you can always begin again.

Some people fail to move toward their goals because of a lack of skill or training, self-doubt, fear of error, or anticipation of opposition. You can never achieve your objectives unless you *act*, and if you fail at a task, obtain information that will help you improve and move progressively closer to your goal the next time around.

PERIODIC SELF-ASSESSMENT

A pruning of outdated habits, along with continual adjustments to keep on target, can ensure progress toward your goal.

Don't, however, become excessively alert to obstacles, accentuating their significance and overcompensating with unproductive diversionary activities, like a blocked writer who becomes preoccupied with sharpening pencils. Excessive concern with details, along with compulsive efforts to prevent errors, can actually lead to paralysis of action.

Preoccupation with detail can also create boredom, tension, and a need to switch activities constantly to generate excitement. What you must learn is how to concentrate on the overall picture of your progress, instead of getting bogged down by the minor slips along the way. Remember that no one ever accomplishes anything without a few missteps and blind alleys. The wise searcher for himself or herself uses those "mistakes" to generate new, improved attempts toward the goal. Periodic assessment involves asking yourself not "What am I doing wrong?" but "What can I learn from that latest slip?"

Mistakes cannot be avoided. What can be avoided is repetition of the same mistakes.

IGNORING THE COMPETITION

I knew a young poet a few years ago whose work, although quite accomplished in itself, was mired in comparison. Not only was most of his poetry stuffed with references to other poets, and especially to the great poets of the past, but the young man's very opinion of his work was a constant comparison with the productions of the great ones—"my masters," he used to call them. The commendable humility of this designation aside, it actually disguised a deep-seated feeling of inferiority about his work vis-à-vis theirs. He could not write a sonnet without observing how it was "not quite up" to a sonnet by Shakespeare or Spenser; he could not do a couplet without bringing in Alexander Pope for comparison; and he shied away from free verse altogether because "Eliot did it so much better."

So indebted was this young poet to the incomparable productions of the past that he was unable to work in the present. Comparison, which had started out as a prod to more serious labor, became in the end a millstone around his poetic neck—a taunt that told him only one thing: he was "not as good" as the masters.

Eventually he stopped writing altogether—which was a shame because had he been able to look at his poetry as *his* poetry rather than a pale imitation of theirs, he might have prospered as a poet. As it was, his unrealistic attempt to compete with the greats of the past led him only into inactivity and frustration.

Paying too much attention to others who are engaged in similar pursuits may encourage envy and self-doubt and lead you to overlook resources available to you alone. It can result in paralysis.

Failure to pursue goals may also result from others' reinforcing your negative self-image because of their *own* anxieties or limited imagination. "So-and-so won't like this" or "You've never done this before" can thus become convenient rationalizations for inaction.

Defining your goal in specific terms can help you avoid becoming involved in the type of distorted and unrealistic expectations that plagued my poet friend. So distracted was he by the notions and productions of others that he lost sight of his initial goal, which was to write good poetry. In pursuing your goal, therefore, few qualities can be as helpful as single-mindedness, or what the old Yankee philosophers used to call "stick-to-itiveness."

ONE DAY AT A TIME

How many times have you heard someone say, "If only I hadn't done such-and-such . . ."?

Such a comment, while perfectly understandable in terms of the necessity of mistakes, is actually one of the most fully useless observations that any of us ever make about ourselves. Recrimination is a dead-end street; you should strive to cut the amount of mooning over lost possibilities in your life to an absolute minimum.

People generally make two principal errors in assessing their daily accomplishments. One is to focus obsessively on how past events have made it impossible for them to act freely in the present. The other is to waste time and energy in fantasy about a golden, untroubled future.

What these two errors have in common is a faulty assessment of the place of time in human affairs.

Now, while philosophers have debated for centuries (without reaching a conclusion) about the nature of time, for a psychologist the question of time is a practical one. The issue really is "How can I best use this day?" Not yesterday, nor tomorrow, but *today*. Keeping your long-range goals in mind, you must pursue immediate activities as if they were the only thing that mattered. Because, in a way, they are.

The Roman emperor Tiberius, an anomaly among Rome's vicious leaders, was known as one of the "good" emperors. So wide was his reputation for good deeds, in fact, that there is a story told of him that once, after finding no one in need of an imperial favor all day, he exlaimed in horror upon retiring, "Alas, I have wasted a day!"

The accuracy of that story may be in doubt, but its moral is not. Tiberius was rare among his contemporaries (indeed, among human beings in general) in recognizing a cogent philosophical truth: this day will last until sunset, no longer. Therefore, if you wish to take advantage of it, you must act *now*. Don't spend time musing on what you *might* have done, but look around you for the opportunities of the moment. Only by doing that can you take full charge of your life in the present.

Start each day with a specific set of objectives to be accomplished *that* day. And end the day by determining how well you have fulfilled them. Undoubtedly you will find that, on most days, you will have accomplished less than you hoped to. But as long as you insist on weighing only the particular possibilities of the day itself, and not the fogs of memory or hope, you will be surprised at how much you *have* accomplished.

Postponing action can be just as debilitating as mooning

over lost possibilities. It ensures, in fact, that the quota of those lost possibilities will continue to grow.

Jane Addams, the founder of the Chicago social service agency Hull House, speaks in her autobiography of "the snare of preparation." People spend so much time, she observed, in *getting ready* to do something that they often discover to their dismay that when the time comes actually to do it, it is too late. Like the writer sharpening pencils, they are left with a handful of perfectly prepared tools and nothing written down.

Learning to act one day at a time means learning to act now as much as it means learning to forget about your damaged yesterdays.

Postponement raises the potential for anxiety about your project, and it gives you more time to contemplate the possible reactions of others. Delay leads only to more delay. It makes tomorrows only one more lost yesterday.

I am not suggesting that you hurl yourself pell-mell into the pursuit of your goals without pausing to look back. New information or developments might require evaluation; they should be judged against your past experience as well as your objectives. They should not be accepted or acted upon impulsively. But in general, if you want to get anywhere, you must take the initial step.

YOU AND OTHERS

None of us lives entirely alone, and one of the most difficult things for a person reorganizing his or her life to do is to gauge where personal goals overlap with those of others and where either they do not touch or they conflict. Since you can never count on other people being supportive when you need support, you must learn to identify what is yours, what you can share with another human being in general, and what you can share only with a few special friends.

Inevitably, you will make errors in judgment on this account, and that will create conflict. You may have formulated a clear-cut life plan, and you may be proceeding fluidly on your path, but what if others interfere by criticizing you? Should you try to get them to stop?

Probably not. It's far better to bypass roadblocks than to waste your energy in conflict.

Besides, when you try to change others, you are trying to manipulate them. This usually intensifies their obstructive behavior—which, of course, intensifies *your* anxiety.

Determine your own responsibilities. To decide what others should do is presumptuous, if not impossible. Your own resentment when others try to impose their standards on you should indicate the futility of such an attempt.

Even if others continually put you down, resist the inclination to retaliate. Instead, try to figure out what you might be doing to make them uncomfortable and insecure. Are you provoking their hostility by setting limits on them? Are you eliciting negative responses by approaching them with negative expectations? If so, you can change.

Ultimately, the strongest relationships emerge from a mutual acceptance and sharing of different interests and abilities.

BECOMING INNER-DIRECTED

A fortified sense of inner-directedness is an integral part of a successful life strategy program.° It will help you develop the confidence that can give you some sense of certainty in an ever-changing world.

If you depend on external cues as guidelines for action, you'll find yourself continually adapting to new cues, new

---

° For information about Life Strategy Workshops in your city, write to Life Strategy Workshops, P.O. Box 1123, Englewood Cliffs, New Jersey 07632.

stimuli, and new expectations, and these actually may be invitations to confusion and distress. Inner-directedness, on the other hand, gives you a firm standard by which to assess the cues of others.

By learning to rely on yourself rather than on others, you'll become less tempted to shift your behavior and goals to accommodate fluctuating social situations. Don't, for example, be afraid to say no to requests that might distract you from what you regard as important.

Inner-directedness and single-mindedness in the pursuit of your goals does not mean, of course, that you must isolate yourself entirely. People *do* need to interact with each other, but you should not do so simply out of dependency or desperation. Ideally, you should be able to pursue your own objectives without slighting the needs of others.

As you recognize your own abilities and interests, you will have less need to depend on others to accomplish what you can accomplish yourself. Being more confident, you will also be less likely to be disappointed by others. Furthermore, you will develop greater sensitivity to the special abilities of others and discover new areas for genuine cooperation. If you are confidently inner-directed, you'll find that you are more tolerant of differences and more inclined to influence others by changing your own behavior (the confident person can do that without fear) instead of by making demands that they change theirs.

The result should be more realistic relationships and the growth of a genuine selflessness. As an inner-directed person, you don't need to impose your needs on others but can invite those with similar needs and interests to participate in shared efforts.

You should be especially careful, however, not to forget the uses of solitude.

As vital as supportive relationships are to you when you are depressed, moments of solitude can also be invaluable—especially if occasional withdrawal lessens the demands being made on you and thus reduces pressure and anxiety.

RELATING TO OTHERS POSITIVELY

Focusing on your goals single-mindedly, becoming inner-directed, withdrawing into yourself, and taking responsibility for yourself do not provide justification for saying "Hooray for me, and the devil with everybody else!"

You can relate to others in *positive* ways without compromising your uniqueness or your goals, so long as you follow these precepts:

1. Be willing to risk changing the way you relate to others, regardless of whether they will accept, reject, ridicule, or rebuff you.

2. Don't be afraid to respond to the needs of others without regard to what's in it for you. Genuine giving is not done out of a sense obligation, but out of a willingness to help.

3. Seek the positive in others. Allow others to feel important—even if they do not respond in kind. Of the several ways in which you can respond comfortably to a situation without compromising yourself, consciously select the one that takes the other person's feelings into consideration.

4. Avoid argument, criticism, boasting, and domination of others. Don't nitpick or focus excessively on problems and difficulties. Concentrate instead on the positive features of an individual's personality, performance, or behavior.

5. Before acting, figure out the best way to pursue your own objectives without limiting the freedom of others.

In the final analysis, each person controls only himself. Modify that which you can control—your own behavior. At best, you can only help others to help themselves. Be careful to avoid direct, unsolicited advice; people rarely appreciate it.

When you progress to the point where you can take full responsibility for your life, when you feel free to ask for what you want without waiting for someone to offer it to you, when you feel free to act without waiting for someone to say it's all right for you to do so, when you have the power to change and the strength to be what you truly want to be—your life will then be too precious for you to want to end it, and you will know the full meaning of the courage to live.

WHAT HAVE YOU GOT TO LOSE?

This has been a book about suicide, and depression, and about the numerous ways in which human beings fight against their own best interests and draw rigid lines around themselves.

We have examined some of the reasons that people enter depressions, and discussed the range of treatments that are now available to contend with this extremely common emotional disorder. We have seen that with chemotherapy and psychotherapy it is possible to abolish more grievous symptoms of depression and enable depressed people to begin to make the decisions that govern their own lives and the directions in which they wish to put their energies. And we have given some attention to some of the myriad ways in which people limit and obstruct their own lives short of actual suicide, and suggested ways in which these people, too, can be helped to realize their full potential and cease standing, as it were, in their own paths.

Before closing I want to return to an image I introduced at the beginning of this chapter, and try to see again how a reluctance to take steps in your own behalf can restrict the possibilities of your life, while a willingness to take the responsibility for your life, even if it means taking chances, can enrich and redefine it.

Imagine again that you are the man in the oasis. Before you is a spring of fresh water, which, after some consideration, you have sampled and found refreshing. All around you, from horizon to horizon, stretch the endless sands. Somewhere beyond them, you have been led to understand, are the settlements and fires of other human beings.

You are confronted, then, by a dilemma.

The way across the sands is sure to be arduous and dangerous. Should you attempt to walk to a settlement, you will almost certainly have to undergo immense privation, including hunger, thirst, exposure, and perhaps death. There is no guarantee, once you leave the relative safety of the oasis, that you will end up as anything but bones for the scavengers.

But what can keep you here?

The oasis contains water, it is true, and shelter under the palms from the merciless desert sun. Perhaps in the tallest reaches of the trees you can even come up with a date or two—if you can climb that far. But clearly there is not enough, even in this pleasantly shaded spot, to sustain life for very long. You cannot live forever on dates and water, and you know it. Eventually, if you stay here, you will die.

It's not an easy choice. On the one hand the burning sands; on the other, a slow death from malnutrition.

What do you do?

I mean to indicate, by this inexact analogy, the dilemma facing any person in a severely depressed state who is offered, through the difficult road of therapy, a chance to change his or her situation. For the suicidal individual, the options may look no more inviting than the options facing our hypothetical hero or heroine in the desert. On the one hand, a tricky journey into increased responsibilities, increased risk; on the other, more of the same.

The wise decision, however, it seems to me, is clear. Between the prospect of a dubious future and no future at all, there is really very little to choose. While inertia and a lifetime of self-depreciation may make it seem much easier to stay in the oasis, in fact it will obviously be easier in the long run (and even in the short run) to take the gambler's leap and start hoofing it into the sands.

The worst that can happen to you, if you choose thus to take charge of your own life, is that you will fail to reach your goal and die, disappointed, somewhere between the oasis and your destination.

And that, after all, is not any worse than the fate that awaits you, disguised as comfort, in the oasis itself.

Is it not therefore better to take the risk, to jump into a possible salvation, instead of waiting around for what you know will wear you down in the end?

In other words, what do you have to lose?

Your life?

Yes, but by remaining a prisoner of the oasis, a prisoner of your old habits and recriminations, you are killing yourself, anyway. So what's the difference, finally?

I do not mean to suggest that there is no difference between letting yourself waste away and offering yourself to the sands. What I want to emphasize is that if you have come to the point of considering suicide, you might as well adopt the behavior that will give you a running chance against your own self-destruction, instead of lying down and allowing it to take you unawares.

If you have the determination to accept the *inevitability* of your own destruction—and we all are bound to die eventually—then you may as well meet it halfway. There is nothing to be gained from merely *waiting* to die. With a slightly different perspective, you can confront the ultimate alertly and consciously. You can take charge of your own life—but let that determination work *for* rather than *against* you!

You can, that is, transform your own destructive impulses into positive, life-changing ones. Energy is malleable; you can have it work *for* you.

Sure, you may not make it.

But if you don't make it, you will at least have died in charge—the director rather than receptor of your life.

Failure is a constant possibility in human affairs. To refuse to seize the opportunity for your own salvation, to refuse to let others, including therapists, help you to a better awareness of yourself, is to allow events beyond your control to take over. No one has ever profited from that kind of inaction.

If you have the courage to contemplate suicide, then you also have the courage to make a different, life-affirming choice. You can choose to give up your choices—or to affirm them by confronting the sands, by taking a conscious part in molding the direction of your experience.

What, finally, do you have to lose?

APPENDIX A

Guidelines for Patients on Chemotherapy

1. Don't become discouraged if results seem slow in coming. Don't blame yourself for what is happening, but regard your depression as you would any other illness.

2. Follow your doctor's instructions to the letter. Inadequate attention to his or her recommendations may not only delay recovery but even *prevent* it.

3. Don't stop taking your medication, and don't decrease or increase the dose unless directed to do so by your physician.

4. Keep a record of all medication taken. Should you have to take other medication prescribed by another physician, surgeon, dentist, or optometrist, such a record should be shown to him or her. This will prevent undesirable mixtures of drugs and will ensure that the appearance of drug-induced side effects, if any, will be understood.

5. *Avoid all forms of alcohol*. This is a *must*. Alcohol may produce undesirable side effects or complications that

may diminish the effectiveness of your medication. In combination with certain drugs alcohol can be lethal.

6. Certain foods, too, must be avoided when taking some types of antidepressants. It is important to follow the recommendations of your physician in such matters.

7. Report any new or unusual symptom to your doctor—no matter how unrelated it may seem to your condition or how easily explained it may appear to be. Such a symptom could be a side effect of the drug you're taking. It's important that you make your physician aware of this so the medication can be adjusted accordingly.

8. Report any significant change of mood, appetite, sleep pattern, energy level, or ability to concentrate.

9. Avoid making any major life changes until you discuss them with your physician. You owe it to yourself and to your doctor to discuss major life decisions during psychotherapy sessions.

10. Don't take on unnecessary burdens while undergoing treatment until it is apparent that you are ready to do so.

11. Above all, do *not* stop seeing your doctor as soon as the medication improves your sense of well-being. Paradoxically, suicidal risk *increases* when a patient's energy level improves to the point of being able to act on suicidal drives. It isn't enough merely to get rid of depressive symptoms; you and your doctor together must work to uncover the *root of your problem.* Only then can you truly develop the courage to live.

APPENDIX B

Guidelines for Selecting a Psychotherapist

Since depression and suicide have both physical and psychological causes, you may prefer to consult a psychiatrist, since psychiatrists are M.D.s with additional training in therapy. As a physician, a psychiatrist can prescribe medication that cannot be prescribed by a nonmedical therapist.

However, there are other types of professionals who can help you solve your problems. They include:

1. Psychologists specifically trained in psychotherapy.
2. Psychoanalysts, among whom are psychiatrists (M.D.s) and psychologists (lay analysts) who have trained at a psychoanalytic institute.
3. Psychiatric nurses with training at a psychotherapy institute.
4. Social workers with training in psychotherapy.
5. Clergymen/women with training in psychotherapy.

How do you find a therapist? The following guidelines may help:

1. First, consider those individuals with whom you are already in contact who may be sources of appropriate referral. For instance, you family doctor already knows a good deal about you and can direct you to a qualified therapist. In addition, your priest, minister, or rabbi, as well as friends in voluntary community agencies who work with the emotionally disturbed, can also be good sources of reference. Another place to start is with a friend who has had a positive experience with treatment and recommends his or her therapist.

2. Your county medical society can give you the names of psychiatrists who specialize in the treatment of depression and the prevention of suicide. Local medical schools will usually offer the names of therapists who are members of the faculty. If there is no medical school in your immediate area, check others in the region. They may have some faculty members living in towns near you. Your local hospitals can also provide the names of psychotherapists on their staffs. Also, check to see if there is a suicide prevention clinic or crisis intervention clinic at these hospitals.

3. Professional societies are also a good source for names of qualified therapists. Among them, the more reputable societies include the American Psychiatric Association, the American Psychological Association, the Society of Clinical Social Work Psychotherapists, and the Academy of Certified Social Workers (ACSW). Your local mental health association may be another source.

4. If you have been referred to a specific individual, *check his or her credentials.* Ideally a psychiatrist should be qualified or certified by the American Board of Psychiatry. (The medical directory for your state, available through your library, lists this information.) A psychologist should be accredited by the American Psychological Association. A social worker should be certified by the ACSW. A psychoanalyst should be affiliated with a psychoanalytic society. Be

wary of anyone calling himself or herself a therapist who lacks proper training and accreditation. There are a vast number of organizations in America that purport to deal with emotional problems. Even though they may have proved helpful to people who want to redefine their lives or learn to think positively, such organizations (and their practitioners) are not really qualified to deal with serious emotional illness.

5. In choosing a therapist, look for compatibility, which is an important factor in long-term psychotherapy—although not so important in immediate crisis intervention. Some methods work better with some kinds of people than with others. The therapist should be someone *you* can talk comfortably with, and whose methods seem compatible with *your* personality. To find out whether the therapist's methods suit you, enter treatment with some provision for an initial trial period. This enables you to assess to what extent you can work productively together.

6. Don't assume that the "experts" necessarily know what is best for you in regard to the amount of distress you can tolerate in the course of treatment. There are many types of treatments available today based on different schools of therapy and emphasizing different degrees of anxiety and uncertainty that may be tolerated by patients. Gauge which one suits you best.

7. During the first few sessions, reach an understanding with your therapist about the specific goals of treatment and the best route to take toward achieving them. Do not assume that the appropriate goals will magically "evolve" over time. Have some idea where you want to go as you begin.

8. Remember that therapists are individual human beings, with not only distinct theoretical approaches to their work, but distinct personalities as well. A therapist may be eminently well qualified and yet absolutely wrong for you. As difficult as it is for you to know what is right for you as

you begin treatment, you must make an effort, for your own preservation, to choose a therapist whose professional and personal identity can best help you discover your own. Ask yourself: "Do I want to spend two or three hours a week talking to this person?" If the answer is no, the therapist's credentials, no matter how good, will be of no benefit to you. And remember that compatibility is to the therapist's advantage as well as to your own. No reputable therapist will pressure a new patient into therapy; the patient-therapist relationships that prove most productive are those where a natural affinity is allowed to develop over time into a solid working commitment to the patient's progress and health.

INDEX